KU-523-604

COMEBACK

COMEBACK

An Actor's Direction

James Fox

Foreword by Dirk Bogarde

HODDER AND STOUGHTON
LONDON SYDNEY AUCKLAND TORONTO

British Library Cataloguing in Publication Data

Fox, James, 1939–
    Comeback. – (Hodder Christian paperback)
    1. Fox, James 1939–   2. Moving-picture
    actors and actresses – Great Britain –
    Biography
    I. Title
    791.43′028′0924   PN2598.F6

    ISBN 0-340-35357-0

Copyright © 1983 by James Fox. First printed in 1983. This edition 1984. All rights reserved. No part of this publication may be reproduced or transmitted in any form or by any means, electronic or mechanical, including photocopy, recording, or any information storage and retrieval system, without permission in writing from the publisher. Printed in Great Britain for Hodder and Stoughton Limited, Mill Road, Dunton Green, Sevenoaks, Kent by Cox & Wyman Limited, Reading. Photoset by Rowland Phototypesetting Limited, Bury St Edmunds, Suffolk. Hodder and Stoughton Editorial Office: 47 Bedford Square, London WC1B 3DP.

CONTENTS

ACKNOWLEDGMENTS

I would like to thank David Stuckey for putting the idea in my mind to write this book and for typing many helpful comments as well as preparing the captions for the photographs.

I would also like to thank Bryan Forbes for permission to quote from his screenplay for the film *King Rat*, based on James Clavell's story, on page 69.

I am grateful to the National Film Archive for their help in providing many of the photographs.

ILLUSTRATIONS

Between pages 64 and 65

James in his pram[1]
James, baby Robert and Edward[1]
Robin Fox[1]
James[1]
The Miniver Story[2]*
The Magnet[3]*
After leaving Harrow[1]
Publicity shot[3]
Photographic session[4]
In the sixties[5]
Passing Tom Courtenay[3]*
King Rat[6]*
Barbed Quartet[6]
In Kenya[1]
The Servant[3]*
The Servant[3]*
Dancing with Julie Andrews[7]*
With James Coburn[1]
Isadora[7]*
Raft scene[1]

Between pages 96 and 97

With Sarah Miles[3]*
With Susannah York[6]*
Those Magnificent Men . . .[8]*
'My Best Role to Date'[9]*
With Mick Jagger[9]*
Performance[9]*

Chas[9]*
Wedding Day[1]
The Navigators[1]
No Longer Alone[10]
The family man[11]
James and his brothers[12]
Angela Fox[13]
Country[14]
Nancy Astor[14]
A Woman for all Time[15]
Love is Old, Love is New[14]

Acknowledgements

* Photographs supplied by the National Film Archive.
  1. Family photographs.
  2. By courtesy of Metro-Goldwyn-Mayer.
  3. By courtesy of EMI.
  4. By courtesy of Terence Donovan.
  5. By courtesy of the Press Association.
  6. By courtesy of Columbia Pictures.
  7. By courtesy of Universal Pictures.
  8. By courtesy of Twentieth Century-Fox.
  9. By courtesy of Warner Brothers.
  10. By courtesy of the Billy Graham Organisation.
  11. By courtesy of Bill Orchard.
  12. By courtesy of David Bailey.
  13. By courtesy of Lord Snowdon.
  14. By courtesy of the B.B.C.
  15. By courtesy of Poseidon Films.

FOREWORD

When I had finished this moving and searingly honest book I realised, I suppose for the very first time clearly, that I had been the catalyst in the story. It was not an altogether comfortable feeling.

One evening at the beginning of the sixties, I turned on as I thought to the news on television. But it was not the news which I saw. I had made an error in selecting the channel and found myself watching the start of a play.

I stayed watching: for one thing the star, Miss Ann Todd, is an actress I greatly admire, and for another the young man playing opposite her was the actor I felt absolutely certain was the one we needed to play an exceptionally important role in a forthcoming film, *The Servant*, which Joseph Losey was to direct and which he was presently trying to cast without much luck. It seemed quite impossible, among the many groups of actors who came to audition for him, to find one who was personable, spoke well and could play, in short, a gentleman. There simply weren't any left as far as we could discover.

It was the time of, what we used to call, the Uglies. Elegance, style, breeding and all that sort of thing had been long since hustled off the stage, and it appeared that every young actor found it essential to look pretty unwashed, ill fed and speak with a flat no-class accent, a mix of harsh North Country and London-Suburban or, even worse than that, just plain Earl's Court-Australian.

It was the time for 'truth' in the theatre and cinema, and 'truth' was almost always ugly, squalid and ill sounding. It was a very monotonous experience: and although a good deal of new theatre and cinema was exciting and stimulating, a lot of it was equally dross, and the harm it caused in the hands of the inexperienced has not been healed today.

However, the young actor I was watching had every single attribute we most needed for the part of Tony in *The Servant*, and above all he could act: there was no question about that at all.

And there was something more. Under the grace and breeding, the golden-boy innocence, I sensed, and I don't for the life of me know why, a muted quality of corruptibility. This young man could spoil like peaches: he could be led to the abyss. Perhaps the most important qualifications for the role. I had never seen him before, didn't know his name, but there was no question in my mind that evening that he was perfect. We had found the ideal Tony. I immediately alerted Losey and asked him to switch on and watch, and telephoned my agent, Robin Fox, who was trying to assist us in setting the film up and who was also a man of great theatrical knowledge. Robin said, politely, that he was already watching the play because the young actor was, in fact, his son. The rest of the story is in this book.

James Fox, as he was to become (his given name, and the one under which I have known him for many years, is William or Will for short), shot to stardom in *The Servant* instantly. It was rather like the take-off, or launching, of a space-shuttle in its splendour and speed, and it spun him high into orbit among the galaxies of stars. Precisely because he was *not* an Ugly, because he could speak correctly, was alert, eager, 'different', he cornered a market. Hollywood was his for the taking: and he took.

The sixties are now known as the years when we 'Never Had It So Good', and for many they certainly were: and James Fox was in the centre surrounded by glittering toys and Pretty People. It was the big breakthrough time for youth; or so it believed, and anything went, and anything did. Everything was possible, nothing impossible; it was all up for grabs and there was absolutely no sign of a tomorrow. For many this was a brutal truth: by the seventies they had burned themselves out and faded away.

But no one thought of this at the time while the pleasure lasted. They were all far too busy breaking old bonds and taboos, throwing off traditions, rules and regulations, removing the ties and restraints, chucking caution to the wind, having fun and seeking some extremely ill defined form of freedom. James sped through the galaxies and the glamour and the fun times, as they were called, as swiftly as an arrow. His mother once remarked, wryly, "Will is the golden star right on the very top of the Christmas tree." And for a time that is how it seemed to be: his course was direct, nothing would deflect it, he was enjoying every moment to the hilt (and sometimes beyond). It was Christmas every day. And jingle bells . . .

As a person he is one of the wittiest I have known; his presence anywhere was marked with laughter and delighted pleasure. He was always the greatest fun to be with, walking across the Downs, sitting round a big log fire, or even at the more boring and tiresome functions which we all had to attend like premieres or press show receptions and so on.

But if he had taken off like a space-shuttle, as he had, then there must be a time for landing: a process of coming down to earth. He could not remain in orbit all his life. As time went on the trajectory of his flight began to alter slowly, and to those of us who knew him well, there were evident signs for concern that all was not absolutely right: something was starting to go very wrong, and he was going off course. There was nothing very much that any of us could do: we watched helplessly as the tumbling shuttle sped away from us towards what one might call a kind of 'desert' landing. A shuddering crash in the barren waste, and the golden star fell from the very top of his Christmas tree into the dust of despair.

But there were two things which some of us had overlooked in the qualities of this tarnished star, alone in the immensity of his own personal desert; and those were his courage and his guts. These had not left him, and with both still amazingly intact he managed, on his own, in his own way, to find his feet and seek the spiritual salvation which he so desperately needed: just in time.

He also found the woman who was to become his wife,

'as summery as a sweet william', and was to help him in his fight for strength, to stand upright once more with pride, and to step out on a path filled with light.

You may well say, 'Oh! It's the old, old story all over again.' And I suppose that you could be right. It has been written and played a million trillion times, and there are, I am informed, only seven basic plots anyway: but this is one of the better ones and has a rather different ending than most.

James Fox is now back where he belongs, in life and in his profession, a glowing future ahead as an actor, none of his essential qualities lost, merely strengthened, and now, with this book, another string to his already strong bow.

How's that for a happy ending?

Welcome back, Will.

DIRK BOGARDE

*To
Mary*

FIRST IMPRESSIONS

It was a summer's day in 1944. My brother Edward and I were picking blackberries on the golf links near our home at Cuckfield in Sussex. Suddenly, from the direction of the South Downs, we heard the powerful drone of a German V1 'pilotless plane'. Then the missile, with its short, stubby wings, came into sight, heading, it seemed, straight towards us. At the same moment a British fighter, a single-engined plane, came from the direction of Shoreham.

Before the missile could reach the spot where we fled for safety in a ditch beneath a hedge, the fighter crept close to it, edged it with its wing on to its side, and hastened its descent into the safe folds of the Ditchling Downs. Its drone became a whine, then followed the impact with the ground and an ascending column of white smoke. We resumed our blackberrying, but the careers of two young actors-to-be had come pretty close to ending before they had begun.

I was born a few months before the outbreak of World War Two, of comfortable theatrical stock, near the banks of the River Thames, the second child of Robin and Angela Fox of Cheyne Walk, London S.W.1.

My first memories of my father were not until I was five years old, as he was called up into the army and spent most of the war with the Royal Artillery shelling the Germans. I don't know what he thought of the war, because he never spoke about it to us, but he collected the MC and a splendid medal called the *Virtuti Militari* from the Poles, which made me extremely proud of him. He also collected a large wound behind his right shoulder blade which he told me had been made by a giant spider. I was rather proud of this too.

My father had some most romantic and heroic antecedents. His mother was the serene Hilda Hanbury, a lady who trod the boards in the days of her more notable sister, Lily, but later gave up acting in favour of married life.

My grandfather was heir to the fortunes of Samson Fox of Bradford, a Victorian engineer and ironmaster of no education, who rose in life to found the Leeds Forge, invent the corrugated furnace flue in 1877 and become three times Mayor of Harrogate. One of his enlightened bequests was a gift of £45,000 for the building of the Royal College of Music in Kensington. Grandpa Willie and Hilda had separated when their children were growing up and he married again, spending his life in travel and sport with rich or aristocratic friends.

I visited him often at his hotel, when he was in his eighties and was fascinated by his exquisite taste in clothes and the devoted cosseting of his French maid, Rose. I remember his favourite topic of conversation being the number of grouse he had bagged in Scotland between 1900 and 1903.

Unfortunately all the care he lavished upon himself left my parents with little more than a mixture of memories. His fortune disappeared up the chimney as rapidly as it had been created. Thus my father, having no great estates to run himself, turned his sharp mind to the legal profession. He had just qualified as a solicitor when duty called him from the circle of his young family into the grim business of killing the enemy.

My father had two sisters and a brother. Mary, the eldest, became bailiff of Lawhyre Farm at Fowey in Cornwall during the war and lived there with my grandmother until she retired. A natural countrywoman, she ploughed with a team of horses, won prizes with her bulls and became an expert at fishing. My father's elder brother, Kenneth, is a renowned trout flytier and has a great love of the countryside, as does the younger sister, Pam, who wrote a book, *All Good Things Around Us*, about the art of using wild flowers and leaves in cookery.

My mother's background was equally unusual and colourful. Her mother was the wife of the much loved doctor of Birchington in Kent, but her father was the famous 1920s playwright, Freddie Lonsdale, by whom my grandmother had two other daughters. Early on, my mother herself became an actress but, like my father's mother, gave up her career when she married and had children; first Edward in 1937, then myself and finally in the spring of 1952, my younger brother Robert.

I was in fact christened William, probably after my grandfather, and was called William while at school. In later years when I became an actor I took the name James under the Equity ruling which tries to avoid two actors having similar names.

When war broke out my mother moved first to Bolney and then to a small cottage in the High Street in Cuckfield in Sussex, a moderately large village on the busy A272, fifteen miles north of Brighton and facing the slim spine of the South Downs as it crests the horizon. My earliest memories are of walks, of jolly and kind helpers and of the chatter of visitors from the army. The Bren-gun carriers rumbled through the village, and my mother says she was ready to put a pillow over our faces if she thought the Germans were successful in landing on the south coast. However, the nearest the war came to Edward and me was that summer's afternoon on the golf links.

Our companions on that walk were 'Al' and her daughter Rosemary and my Aunt Yvonne. Alice Mitchell – Al to us – had been trained in service with her sister Edie on one of the big Norfolk estates and had come to Bolney, where she met my mother, after her husband died. She then came to live with us in the cottage and helped my mother with the cooking and with us children. She was expert in Irish stews, shepherd's pies, chocolate cake and treacle tarts, and was naturally very popular.

Edie, her sister, lived in Brighton and took the No. 14 bus from there to Cuckfield – an hour's journey each way – once a week to mend, iron and generally look after our clothes. She was a gentle and thorough woman, and I enjoyed their company very much, especially on our long walks in the rich woods around the village, primrosing and blackberrying.

In the immediate post-war years my father began a new career with the American theatrical agency, MCA, and travelled up to London by train. I was slightly in awe of him. I used to watch his morning shave, fascinated by the clean swathes of polished skin appearing across his handsome face. Money wasn't plentiful, but my mother had a great ability to find all sorts of helpers for the house and garden who were rewarded by her enthusiasm and a 'nip' on Saturday morning.

Our home was sometimes a sort of extension of a West End manager's office, constantly interrupted by phone calls and the intrusion of the famous; always a script to read over the weekend; always alive with news, opinions, criticisms of plays and performers and talk of the business; thriving on creativity and the needs of creative people, which can never be satisfied.

My parents often went to the Theatre Royal in Brighton on Saturday night to see a play – usually one which had a client or a friend in it. In this way I developed the expensive habit of viewing plays from about the seventh row of the stalls.

Afterwards we would go backstage and visit the star, usually Robert Morley. Robert would greet us, "Well dear, is it going to do? Do you think we'll be in the money with this one?"

My father would mention something about the third act or a certain actor.

Robert's eyebrows would go up. "I know, dovekins. She can't do it, can she? We'll have to think of something, won't we? Now, what about a lovely dinner? Wheeler's? Yes. Come along, Ros." Ros was his stage manager and later my agent. "William dear. How's school? – Dreadful? – I know – your father still wears his old Harrovian tie, having hated every minute of it and somehow thinks it'll change his

sons for the better. Aren't you hungry? Come along, everyone."

We would then troop out behind this generous and
gigantic star, feeling better for his wit and his company. In
the car, on the dark roads back to Cuckfield, my father
would carry on, imitating Robert's voice exactly, as he and
my mother went over the things the play would need before
it came into the West End.

In contrast to this rarefied theatrical atmosphere my
mother had a number of local friends from non-theatrical
backgrounds, whose homes we visited to play with their
children. Tommy Fairfax-Ross was a member of the royal
household. He and his wife 'Flick' had a daughter Christine
who was our age. They rode horses and had a drive, a
Horsham tile-roofed house, a wooden hall, pictures of
soldiers and huntsmen on their dining-room walls and a real
upstairs nursery with a rocking horse, a doll's house and a
permanent nanny.

Pam and David Manwaring-Robertson had two sons our
own age with whom we gave a children's dance. It was a
great success. In fact, we went to a lot of children's dances
locally, graduating from best suits from Rose's in Bond
Street to dinner jackets. We were always well turned out and
my mother insisted that we write 'thank you' letters afterwards.

Ernest and Joan Kleinwort were bankers. They had a
swimming pool, a garden full of rhododendrons and a
tennis court where my father would play tennis, with his
unforgettable serves, beautifully wound up and heavily
sliced.

The General and Molly Brocas-Burrows also had a drive
to their house. Indeed, I felt rather apologetic when they
came to our house and had only a garden path to walk up.
Their sons, Richard and Michael, were Etonians, and I
adored their sporting brilliance and elegance.

But soon it was time for my first boarding school, Ashfold
School at Handcross. Later I came to like school, but my
first memories at seven were of tears, dormitories called by

colours (my first, Purple) and strangeness. Ashfold was a handsome Elizabethan-style manor house at the end of a beech and playing-field-lined drive, with mullioned windows, an oak front door and the smell of floor-cleaning wax to greet its new arrivals.

Its headmaster was Jim Harrison, in tripartite management with Dick Sykes and Mr Seccombe. The best thing about the school was that it was comparatively easy going. One of my friends, David Sieff, was keen on racing, ran a book, and tried to hustle some bets from the staff. He was not discouraged. Work, sport and enjoying ourselves were given equal importance. Boys were allowed to do their own thing, even to the extent of masters watching indifferently from the terrace as boys scaled the topmost branches of mature beech trees.

My first real interest in life came about through this craze for tree climbing. My imagination was fired by the exploits of C. S. Forester's Captain Hornblower. One of the boys, Bolton, got our dormitory reading his books. My favourite was the one in which Hornblower was a lieutenant with the *Lydia* and met and fell in love with Lady Barbara.

Bolton fulfilled his Hornblower fantasy by building a treetop version of the *Lydia* in a large beech tree. On our estate-work afternoons boarding parties of boys hurled cold Sussex clay up on to the decks and then made aloft. But the best part was to be with Bolton in blue dungarees on his quarter-deck, pretending to be Mr Bush, who had had his leg shot off by a Spanish cannonball, sending gruff orders to his men to 'belay' and urging us to fire back with our own mud supply. These adventures were much more satisfying than being in the school play. In fact, I never enjoyed theatricals very much when I was at school.

At Ashfold I had my first emotional crush on another boy, behaving very furtively on a bus on the way back from a youth concert in London. It was all very intense. Homosexuality was hardly rampant but it was there and probably inevitable among seven to twelve year olds confined together for thirty weeks of the year. As we discovered our sexual feelings, we also had fun trying to catch the junior masters and the young matrons whom we imagined were having a torrid scene. Sure that we were stalking lovers through the rhododendron woods, we always ended up disappointed.

I enjoyed history but was bored by geography – filling names on an empty map of the world and writing about the artesian well. Likewise I was permanently confused in maths, but was much more interested in the teacher, Miss Horne's, masculine hairstyle and rough tweeds.

English grammar bogged me down. But I woke up the moment we came across *Beau Geste*. Jim Harrison read this classic boys' story to us on Sunday evenings and I shall never forget the pleasure of sitting, in our dressing gowns, around him as the exciting Foreign Legion drama unfolded.

Jim Harrison taught Latin, which I couldn't get along with either, but it was made pleasurable because he taught it. I enjoyed watching his red pen obliterate my work, as I stood by his big chair and saw the twinkle in his eye as he gave it back to me. At sport, my best game was cricket, once triumphing by bowling out ten men in one innings. But above every other pleasure, I was fond of home.

Once I ordered the village taxi to come and fetch me and a friend for a day out. We went to my home, found my mother away, and were enjoying some of Al's shepherd's pie, when the phone rang. Mr Sykes was furious and beat me with a slipper for my escapade – though I couldn't see what the fuss was about.

It was the holidays that I really longed for, to see my dog Danny and my friend Robin Edwards. Our interests were sport and traditional jazz. We invented a game of garden cricket with a small bat and a golf ball. We became expert at Subbuteo table football, watched Sussex play cricket and supported Brighton and Hove Albion and Cuckfield Football Club.

Next to our house was the village baker's shop. We liked the baker and his bread, but he had a rather severe van driver who loathed us. One Sunday my friend and I discovered some stink bombs on sale in another village shop. We experimented with a few and found them to be truly rotten-egg nasty. But how could we target them in the most satisfying way? We decided on the baker's shop, went in and bought two jam tarts. Under cover of this innocent operation we crushed the glass capsules and made our escape. Outside the door we ran like mad into our house and to an upstairs window to see if anyone would explode out of the shop. Unfortunately, all remained quiet. However, the escapade achieved some notoriety and I am still known in Cuckfield for this prank thirty-five years later.

Robin's father became keen on roses, so the garden cricket had to stop and we took up jazz more keenly. Robin played the clarinet and I tried the trombone. We became Humphrey Lyttleton fans. My first LP was a ten-inch record of Jelly Roll Morton's Red Hot Peppers.

Then we acquired a new friend called Brian, the curate's son, who was older. With his help we managed to meet a girl called Sylvia, and took it in turns to go behind a tree in the park and kiss her.

My father's career was prospering and he was united with stars like John Mills, Robert Morley, David Niven, Douglas Fairbanks Jnr, Gladys Cooper, Audrey Hepburn, and directors like Wendy Toye and Terence Young. His closest theatrical relationship continued to be with Robert Morley. He represented him as an actor, playwright and cabaret star and was his best audience. Robert repaid him with generosity and an interest in all of us.

From an early age I was adept at mixing a Sunday morning pink gin and handing round the smoked salmon sandwiches to the many guests who crammed into our laughter and smoke-filled cottage drawing room. These gatherings followed church. We used to huddle together in the beautiful village church, amid its sombre echoes and the timid twitterings of the village choir.

If my mother and father had any religious interest, I think they were attracted towards Zionism. My father was one-eighth Jewish and very proud of it. Even I could see that our

Jewish friends managed to combine the religious and secular more naturally in their lives.

My father and mother's closest friends were Michael and Daphne Sieff. They had known the Sieff, the Marks and the Blond families since their teens and attributed their taste and education in art, music and hospitality to this remarkable Jewish family, which had founded and now ran Marks and Spencer.

I spent many a Sunday with my parents at the Blonds' watching my father play bridge and listening to my mother and her friends. It was there that I heard my first LPs of the Broadway musicals – *Guys and Dolls*, *South Pacific* and *Annie Get Your Gun*. My brother Edward once said regarding these patriarchs that if you took them out of their English country-house setting, you could quite easily imagine them alighting from a camel instead of the Rolls.

Like the Sieffs' commitment to retailing, my parents' involvement in the theatre was more than a job. One day my father took Edward and me to the MGM studios at Borehamwood to see a client. We met the head of casting, Irene Howard, and visited the set where they were making *The Miniver Story*, a sequel to the popular wartime film *Mrs Miniver*, with Greer Garson and Walter Pidgeon.

We went through the great heavy padded double doors into the dark cavernous hangar where the action was and were greeted by commanding shouts for "Quiet!" A red light over the door and a bell gave the signal for all work to cease and then the set was sealed. We crept closer to the camera; the camera crew waited. The first assistant continued to shout for silence. A lighting cameraman looked through a piece of darkened glass, instructing his assistant with orders to the gantry above.

"Close the inky . . . open the barn doors a fraction . . ."

The scene before us was bathed in light; the spectators were in the dark. The hairdresser moved in to Greer Garson's hair, beautifully groomed under a plastic rainhat. Shrubbery grew out of the cables littering the floor. A giant hose coiled around our feet.

"Let's have the water . . . stand by!"

The clapperboy advanced with his small blackboard, the hoses squirted into life, the arc lamps spluttered into dazzling fire. The deluge, focused on to Mrs Miniver's garden path and parked car, began. The camera, mounted on a carriage on long rails, began to move.

"Turn over . . . action!"

Mrs Miniver ducked out of the car and made her way, under her umbrella, up the garden path. "Right, cut it," shouted the first assistant, and we were hustled towards the tea urn in the dark corner where we sipped and watched.

After our tea we were introduced to Greer and the director. They both seemed remarkably taken with us and wanted to know if one of us would like to do a little screen test for the part of Mrs Miniver's eleven-year-old son, not yet cast. Edward was shy, but I jumped at the invitation and was prepared for the test with Greer.

I can't remember the exact details of my part but I think I had to come in from school with a raging hunger and ask my mum what was for tea. Then I picked up a baseball bat and swung it just as my 'father', Walter Pidgeon, came in. I almost knocked him over. I'm told I handled the words and the props so well that he said to someone, "There go my notices."

I enjoyed it enormously and felt entirely happy to pretend that this glamorous red-haired lady was my mother. I think I was offered the part immediately. Hushed and awed, we retired again through the heavy netted doors and out into the draughty covered way between the giant stages, unable to speak. I was held by the intensity of my new experience, hooked on becoming a film actor then and thereafter.

Duly engaged for the part, my joy was made complete by the promise of a three-speed bike. It only remained for me to be extricated from Ashfold and installed in the Berkeley Hotel for the period of shooting. This must have been for about three weeks. I believe the school were willing to let me do some film acting, but I don't know how they felt about my success in *The Miniver Story*, which led to my being offered *The Magnet* for Ealing Studios, which would take me out of school for two whole terms the following year.

I was singled out for some favourable mentions in the London daily newspapers and enjoyed my success hugely. The critics talked of my 'endearing fair-haired naturalness', though one, I remember, hoped he would never see me or any other child star again.

The Magnet was a film about a young boy from Birkenhead near Liverpool who deceives a child on the beach into giving him his giant magnet. Then, believing he is going to be arrested for the crime, he guiltily runs away from home, fetching up with a gang of rough young Liverpudlians, until eventually he is returned to his worried parents.

It was lovingly directed by Charles Frend who did *The Cruel Sea* and *Scott of the Antarctic*, written by T. E. B. Clarke of *Lavender Hill Mob* and Ealing comedy fame. The reviews were favourable and large photographs of me appeared in the national newspapers and in advertisements, giving me that heady feeling of being a very important person. Lest this exalted view of myself should become too attractive, my parents explained that I could decide what I wanted to become later, when I had finished my essential schooling. But for the present I had some way to make up if I was to pass exams into Harrow School, and so I was returned to Ashfold.

Back at school, I felt the year's break rather badly – I was treated very well and enjoyed a season in the First XI cricket team and as a prefect. Only a few people let me know they thought I needed squashing. But the biggest loss was in the continuity of friendships broken by the spell away.

In the spring of 1952 my younger brother Robert was born, and after the christening we all gathered together for a star-studded party. There was champagne on the lawn, with Robert Morley and his family, Gladys Cooper, Godfrey Winn (who was my godfather) as well as the Blonds and our local friends, the Fairfax-Rosses and Manwaring-Robertsons. I took some photographs with my camera of the new babe who was at the centre of attention, and the bright guests who surrounded our family.

This was the world I really loved – the world of grown-ups – and I wanted to be included in it. But another world was proposed. I scraped into the fourth form of Harrow School for the autumn term of 1952 and was admitted into Rendalls, which had been my father's house in the mid-1920s. His rather sad expression gazed back at me from the brown-tinted house photograph on the dining-room wall. Could it be that he felt very much as I did now about being a public-school boy?

2

FROM PUBLIC SCHOOL TO DRAMA SCHOOL

The first thing that struck me about starting at Harrow School was that they wanted to make me look different. My first appointment was at the school outfitters, Messrs Gieves. My wardrobe was a weekday blue jacket and grey trousers, soft detached collar and black tie, with the whole thing topped off with the well-known boater (though you'd get sniffed at for calling it that).

On Sundays I had to go the whole way – cutaway tail-coat, high stiff neck-eroding wing collar and striped trousers with a black waistcoat. But the most famous bit of gear at Harrow is the straw hat, which can express its owner's personality by the way it is worn: rakish angle, hair awry (bit of a lad); straw coming adrift (bit brainy); shading the eyes (bit mysterious); worn correctly (must be dodgy).

Underneath the hat in winter was worn a scarf, nine feet long, which could be wound round the neck three times like a snake. A notable games hero or school monitor (prefect) would sport an enviably coloured one. All three buttons of one's blue jacket had to be done up during one's first year. Penalties could be imposed for failure to comply. After a year only the single central button had to be fastened. After two years you could let it flap – and you did, regardless of fashion, weather or comfort.

Within the uniformity, therefore, there were subtle signals reinforcing by means of dress a system of rewards, privilege and position. The acme of this sartorial elegance was one Bloomfield who could sport a speckled straw hat with a crest on the ribbon (indicating school cricket XI and school monitor), plus a ten-foot scarf of dirty white with black stripes (rugby XV) on weekdays, or black bow tie and grey waistcoat with cutaway tails (Philathletic Club) on Sundays. The wardrobe was the message.

Then, once everyone had been made to look the same, we were introduced to the duties of fagging, a system which meant that for a year you were a slave to some of the house monitors. Rendalls had about fifty boys in all. In our intake there were only about seven or eight of us, so we became the slave workforce to the others for a year. There were two duties – general fag and personal fag. You began as a general fag. In response to a long yell of "Boy, boy, boy," you would leave your room at a lick and try not to be the last to reach the caller. A certain familiarity with the caller's intonation and a knowledge of his whereabouts were, along with the acceleration of a Saudia Williams, desirable assets. The slower ones invariably got the job, which usually consisted of taking a note to someone in another house, going and buying a packet of chocolate biscuits, or occasionally something rather more onerous.

Personal fagging came after a term at the school, when you were assigned duties for an individual and were exempt from some general fagging. Then it was a matter of cleaning his shoes and blancoing his corps clothes, making his bed or running his bath, serving him tea, etc. I suppose most boys calculated that a year of this at thirteen would be compensated for by a year of being on the receiving end at seventeen or eighteen, but I'm afraid I was never much motivated by the idea. My own particular senior was called T. D. Wilson Smith. His foible was to insist that I put polish and cleaned in the welts of his shoes.

Fagging is basic to the public-school system. It is designed to diminish the egos of little prep-school boys and to establish rather forcibly the concept of the authority structure. The housemasters keep out of most things to do with running the house while the boys establish a hierarchy within the house based on their length of time at the school.

For instance, after being three years at the school, you automatically became eligible for certain privileges. These entitled you to have access to the house senior boys' private study, to wear a white scarf after lunch, to have a radio, to be exempted from certain roll calls or meal attendance if you wished, to attending a slap-up Sunday morning breakfast, to being in friends' rooms later than a set time, and so on.

Above the three-yearers were the four-yearers and above them the appointed house monitors. At the very top of the tree was the Head of House. His powers even included beating the younger boys for certain offences – and not only younger boys, as I will relate. This system can only work because all the boys are boarders and live in this micro-culture for thirty-four weeks of each year. I felt confined by it, and remember a line from a poem I wrote:

Oh to be in Regent's Park, without my housemaster's permission . . .

The aim of the system, I believe, is to produce independent and experienced young men who are potential leaders. It works well enough if you appreciate what it is trying to achieve, but I never had it explained to me, and would probably have been unwilling to cooperate anyway.

I was behindhand in school work at the beginning and never really got going. One reason for this was that I never found a subject I excelled in, so I settled for modern languages. Most of the teaching didn't get through to me, either. The exception was Mr E. V. C. Plumptre, who taught the classical sixth, but what he introduced me to went far beyond the subjects on the school curriculum.

I first heard from 'Plum' (as he was known) through a postcard in a diagonal scrawl asking me to tea. He was a revered and loved figure in the school and taught Latin and Greek to the classical upper sixth. Apart from that he played in the school orchestra and supervised the Vaughan Library, but kept well clear of the corps or sports, partly, I suppose, due to tuberculosis when young. You could always tell when he was around by his well-known TB cough.

His housekeeper, Margaret, provided a slap-up tea on a trolley and we would sit opposite one another across his fireplace. He played recordings of Dylan Thomas reading his own poetry and gave me Evelyn Waugh to read, but he talked about everything very light-heartedly: travel in Italy and Greece, politics or economic news. He also played Chopin on the piano. He was very shy and shortly due to retire and I suppose I was a pleasant companion for an afternoon.

Our friendship continued as he found out more about my family and background. He encouraged me to enter the playwriting competition for a school prize – the Terence Rattigan Award. I worked out a play which I submitted – and it won. .

In the holidays we went to *Look Back in Anger* in its first production at the Royal Court, which I enjoyed. Then we went to *Waiting for Godot*, which neither of us understood but which we talked about a lot and felt was an important theatrical experience. We even went to the House of Commons together. Plum met my mother and father, and we took him to *Don Giovanni* at Glyndebourne. During my last year at Harrow, Plum was one of its few consolations.

It was compulsory to attend chapel daily and twice on Sundays – a guaranteed way to turn most schoolboys off religion for the rest of their lives. The chaplain was a well-meaning soul but with him the mysteries of the faith remained secure. He had *twuble wiv his r's* and when we went to private confirmation classes with him we spent most of our time trying not to hide under the table.

When the day actually came we were all seated in our rows ready for the Bishop of London to lay his hands on us. It was at that moment that I developed the most uncontrollable giggles which I managed to suppress by furiously biting my lip as I went up to the communion rail. But as I turned and walked back to the pew I had the impression that the whole confirmation class were in convulsions and I dissolved. I could hear the voices of my friends as I climbed over their legs to try and regain my place.

"Twy and contwol yourself, Fox."

"For goodness' sake man, get a gwip on yourself."

"Sowwy, not this woe."

Getting confirmed provided an additional perk. By going to the 8 a.m. Sunday morning communion you could escape the 11 a.m. morning service.

I was no success at rugby or Harrow football, which I felt were very cold and wet activities, but I did develop a liking and a skill for fives and was awarded my school scarf, or colours, playing for the third pair. Fives is a game, invented at Eton College where according to tradition it began, with boys hitting a ball with their hands against the wall of the school chapel and using the buttress as an obstacle and trap. You play it in pairs in an open-ended court wearing padded gloves. In my time in the school team we never had very good results and were usually beaten by other schools. But my house, Rendalls, provided most of the school players and we were house champions.

Along with fives, the other activity our house excelled in was the corps competition, though our success was regarded with some derision by the rest of the school. We won the cup year after year and for several weeks prior to the competition, which was decided on drill and turn-out, we sweated over Kiwi boot polish, Blanco and Duraglit. It did at least come in useful when I did my National Service later.

I must have been unlucky, for my experience in the classrooms was woefully boring. Considering all the money my parents shelled out they got very little value for it in the academic or cultural line. The things that make life interesting were in my case almost totally absent for thirty-four of every fifty-two weeks in a year. No wonder I counted off the days until the holidays.

Despite this, one's loyalty to the school remained fiercely strong and I supported our first teams loudly, especially at the annual Eton and Harrow cricket match at Lords. I would go up into the free seats and shout H-A-R-R-O-W for the blood of the Eton batsmen, except when my friend Richard Burrows was playing for Eton. I was glad to see him make some runs. In my time Harrow usually lost or drew but it was great fun listening to the barracking up at the Nursery End led by Brian Johnston, an old Etonian who mocked our side hilariously.

Adolescence is of course a time of great emotional turbulence and an increasing awareness of things of a physical and sexual nature. How did it affect me? The influence of my family and my dependence on them began to decrease in some respects as I made new friendships, especially with Charles, a boy of great humour and academic ability, and two others from the same intake. None of us much respected the system at that time, and we did not conform to the conventional standards of behaviour that would have guaranteed us success. We took to puffing Benson and Hedges or Sobranie up the chimneys of our small rooms, competing with one another as to who could write the best blue short stories, and mocking our rather earnest superiors.

Most of us were healthily attracted to girls, but the absence of them at public schools made us open to a few homosexual relationships as well. I don't think this caused any tendency towards a permanent homosexual preference but I do think our whole public and private school experience permanently influenced our attitude to and behaviour with girls. After the first kiss behind a tree in the park at about ten and a rather serious attraction for a local girl who rode horses and for whom I bicycled ten miles for a bit of snogging at about thirteen, I did not get to know any girls of my own age very well. I suppose there were opportunities in the holidays but until I went to drama school I don't remember enjoying the friendship or companionship of a girl.

In the holidays, my friends and I, fired by all the imagination and desire of fifteen year olds, worked out our fantasies on West End ladies at three pounds a time. As would be expected these neither gave us a deeply satisfying sexual experience nor increased our appreciation of the opposite sex.

But our preference was for the little scrubbers at Cy Laurie's club in Windmill Street. My friends and I watched them admiringly for hours and then – even better – actually danced with them. You twisted them in a tight whirl under your upheld hand, reeled them out to the end of a long unwinding curve, and then pulled them back to you again to the marvellous trad sounds of Cy Laurie's band.

My friends and I shared intensely in all these experiences and it drew us closely together. But they only served to separate us from the goings-on at the school. At the end of my third year it all blew up. One incident illustrates the strain which began to exist between myself and the authorities.

I was playing fives one afternoon when another boy told me to stop doing something or other or else leave the court. I was a three-yearer and he was a four-yearer in the same house. I told him to "buzz off" and he reported me to the Head of House for saying it. It must have gone quickly up to the housemaster and back to the senior boys in charge because I got a few cool looks at teatime. I conferred with my friends and the feeling was that I would be in for trouble.

After lights out I heard the sinister attenuated call for "B-o-o-o-y!" and lay there thinking: "They wouldn't call me into Reader for that, would they?" (Reader was the library where beatings took place.) I heard the slippered feet of the night boy – "You're wanted in Reader." I jumped down the stairs in my pyjamas and there, solemnly lined up, was the sixth form.

"What have you got to say about your insolence in the fives court?"

It didn't matter much what I had to say; clearly sentence was due to be passed anyway. The cane was visible in the rather beefy hand of our Head of House. I mumbled something. I felt deeply humiliated. I was not a junior, I was sixteen years old, and they were seventeen or eighteen. My heart was racing. I think I blurted out an angry and emotional condemnation of them all.

"Lift up your dressing-gown. Put your head under that table." Six times the beastly whipping cane descended. I held on, not lifting my head until it was over. ". . . And your three-year privileges are taken away. Now go."

Stunned in my brain as well as my bottom I hopped out of the room and down the corridor, fighting my tears and pride and hating the whole wretched establishment. It had become obvious what I was not – the conformist, responsible, house-spirited type – and what I was, or wanted to be, was a free spirit, appreciated and rewarded. But how? The answer had never been far away. I must become a film actor.

Quickly I decided that I should leave the school. My friend Charles was having to leave too. He had developed tuberculosis and was lying in the sanatorium. I didn't *feel* a failure, but I was one.

In Winston Churchill, Harrovians who fail have a very reassuring solace. Among the good things I did carry away from the school are the memories of his visits. The most honoured old boy in living memory would sit huddled on the Speech Room stage, listening to the five hundred boys' voices lustily singing the lilting Victorian school songs, until a great white handkerchief was shaken and applied. Then he would rise feebly, yet project his words firmly when he gave us his gruff appreciation of the power of those same songs when they lifted his spirits in 1941, and how he still found pleasure and encouragement in hearing us sing them. Then he would hobble down some steps and along the High Street, which echoed to our loudest cheers, reflecting our genuine pride in his achievements – and the gratitude we all felt for what he had done for us.

To summarise those four years: I discovered (not then, but much later) that to make progress in anything you have to work. At Harrow I didn't, but I made some good friends. It gave me a context from which to approach life constructively. I learned how to clean shoes and light fires, play Eton Fives and be treated like the dregs.

I don't know what made me want to train as an actor and the results of my time at Central School rather proved that. Acting was something I thought I would be good at. I hadn't found anything to pursue after school and the only world I knew was the theatre. I suppose I fell into it.

Robert Morley did his best to discourage me in a fairly light-hearted way: "William, dear, do you think you should go into acting? It's a very precarious business." But my parents were more resigned.

I think I chose Central because people had said that it was good for voice training. For my audition pieces I sought the help of Bill Squire, an actor who lived in our village, and he heard my modern piece from Anouilh and helped me choose my Shakespeare speech. I went for the audition and was accepted.

My father had taken a flat in Old Burlington Street which he lived in during the week and he let me stay there during my time at drama school. I brought my bike up from the country and used it to get to work. The Central School of Speech and Drama had its home at that time in the Albert Hall, on the balcony level. The facilities were obviously not ideal but they were adequate. Our class was very friendly. I remember them mostly in black tights, for movement class was a major item in the curriculum. We spent a lot of time walking round in a circle to the piano and doing relaxing exercises, flopping our bodies forwards and letting our hands hang down, rolling our heads round in a circle and lying on the floor raising our arms and legs. I still use these exercises for relaxing. We were also introduced to mime. Each of us had to get up and do a mime exercise on our own in front of the class, as well as in groups. One we all enjoyed was pretending we were in a crowded Underground train hanging from a strap. Then we would imagine we were flowers or trees and so on, and our efforts were judged by the teacher.

Having been brought up with an expensive education, I

really didn't think they could teach me much about voice production. Of course I was wrong, but the exercises were of the tongue-twister variety and I quickly became bored.

In the second term we tried our hand at Elizabethan prologues, which are rather an acquired taste. I don't think I was asked to do mine. We also had classes in make-up and the history of costume. For make-up I went and asked advice from Tom Chatto, an experienced actor and Ros's husband.

"Oh, a bit of five and nine is all you need my boy. Perhaps some umber if you have to black up."

I went and bought my sticks of five and nine — sticks of make-up numbered according to lightness and darkness — and mixed them together for the base. I then applied the lighter one to my nose and cheeks and inside my eyelids and the darker one under my jaw. I looked round at my companions. Some of them were now a ruddy hue, while the girls had gone mad round the eyes with strong black pencil lines. To get the awful stuff off you had to grease your face with thick white cream and scrape the remains off with Kleenex. Later we were encouraged to use our sticks to create character.

At the end of our first year we were given a chance to do a Shakespeare play. Ours was *The Winter's Tale* and I was given two roles: Florizel, the handsome young man, and Antigonus, the ancient courtier. The better parts went to the actors who had already distinguished themselves in mime, prologues and make-up where I had come off pretty badly. Florizel was all right and I tried to carry him off with some romantic ardour. But I was stuck with how to get across as Antigonus, especially as we had no costumes to help us beyond the old black tights. Since he was a venerable gentleman of the court I hit on the idea of giving him a stick. But as bad luck would have it our teacher gave me a very long cross from one side of the stage to the other at the same time as I was to deliver my bit of sage advice.

When the day came, I knew it was not going quite right the moment I set off. The stage of the theatre seemed to stretch for miles as I limped my way across the open expanse with everyone standing around looking very interested. I happened to catch the faces of our rival class in the front row as they watched my progress and detected suppressed guffaws. I let my look carry to the adjudicators at the back and I could see their faces in the low desk-lights in front of them, looking serious. It was an awful moment.

As I expected, this particular piece of characterisation received suitable attention when our performances were adjudicated later. Decades later, the memories of that performance crossed my mind when, as the infirm Waldorf Astor in the TV series *The Astors*, I had to walk across the hall at Cliveden and then some way up the drive with a walking stick.

There were some lovely students on our course, and we all became good friends. When we weren't at Central we would go and visit my friend Charles at his parents' home in Sheffield Terrace.

Frankly, however, the drama school was not getting through to me very much – and neither was the London stage. I wasn't a passionate playgoer like a lot of my year though there were certainly some excellent things to see: Scofield in *The Power and the Glory*, *Roar Like a Dove* and lots of interesting plays at the Old Vic. My interest was more in the films that were coming over from America, and Charles and I spent a lot of time in the West End cinema. One of the first we went to was *Blackboard Jungle*, the film that introduced Bill Haley and the Comets singing 'Rock Around the Clock'. It was not only the vibrant music but the gripping story of a reign of classroom terror in a poor urban school that was so good. The acting, the violence and the mood were totally realistic. Charles' brother Gerard had turned us on to the first Elvis Presley LP and we began to wear donkey jackets and very tight black trousers with narrow white stripes.

Charles was painting and writing poetry but he was also a voracious reader. He introduced us to *The Catcher in the*

Rye and we identified with J. D. Salinger's articulate adolescent hero. Another lesser known film that made an impression on us was *A Man is Ten Feet Tall* with Sidney Poitier and Jack Warden. Here again there was antagonism, this time between white and black working men, with the black as the more intelligent and dignified. It was brutal and beautiful.

The great classic of the period was *On The Waterfront*, which produced the best combination of similar themes, with superb acting and direction. Again we were attracted by the vivid naturalism of New York dockland and the toughness and grind of urban life. We sat in awe of the playing of Brando, Steiger and Lee J. Cobb and we longed for the loser Brando to win. Another little known film that we saw at a late night showing at Warners was *End as a Man*, with Ben Gazzara. As a sadistic West Point classman he was a method actor too. *Sweet Smell of Success* was another favourite, a product of the great screenwriter Clifford Odets and the British director Sandy Mackendrick. The action was fast, the dialogue witty. Burt Lancaster and Tony Curtis gave great performances. There were many good lines including, from the fat cop about to beat up the cynical reporter: "Come here, Sidney, I want to chastise you."

All these films were in black and white as was *Twelve Angry Men*, another which was brilliantly acted. One colour film that particularly excited us was *Gunfight at the OK Corral*, which I must have seen several times. It was a film with a lot of action and suspense involving characters you had to love. These films convinced me that I wanted to be a film actor but they also influenced my taste in films. I think we were very fortunate to live in this time of great American creativity in the cinema and I am sure it fertilised a lot of the writing, direction and acting of Britain's film production in the sixties.

What I couldn't see was how my drama-school experience was helping me to become like one of these film actors I admired. I watched the third years doing their fully dressed three-act play for the critics and agents who had come to see them. It was a star-studded cast including Vanessa Redgrave, Judi Dench and Jeremy Kemp, but I wasn't excited by the finished product. I concluded that if that was where the school was leading me I'd better not waste two years there. I told my parents.

My mother had an answer for most of my decisions, "Willie thinks he knows best about everything."

Another factor was that I knew that as soon as I'd finished my second year at Central I was likely to be called up for my National Service. Most of those who were having to do that were considering coming back for their final year when they had completed it. Four years from now – the end. So, not knowing exactly what to do, I left Central.

My father and Robert Morley had just joined together in theatrical management and were mounting their first production, a comedy by Robert Morley, *Six Months Grace*, starring Michael Shepley and Yvonne Arnaud. I was allowed to join the company for the tour as an assistant stage manager – ASM – at six pounds a week. Our opening was at the Alexandra at Birmingham and then after a three week tour we were to open at the Phoenix in London. The play was about what happens when the wives of the directors of a fruit-importing firm decide to do their husbands' jobs for six months and let the men run their homes. It went down rather well and business was good.

My job was to call the cast from their dressing rooms at various times before the performance, check the stage for correct props and settings and sometimes follow the text from the book. I enjoyed watching each performance from the wings and I am sure I was one of the most appreciative audiences.

It was my first experience of touring and living in theatrical digs (weekly lodgings). I must say that although it was novel it didn't strike me as a particularly comfortable existence. We settled down to a run of about six months in London where things got monotonous.

I heard that they were auditioning for a play called *The Happiest Millionaire*. I went along and got offered a small part and also an ASM job in the production, which was possible because my part was only in the first scene. The play was about an American family called Biddle and concerned an eccentric father, who hired a prize-fighter as his sparring partner and kept an alligator. It would seem that the producers had caught this eccentric spirit, because they cast Wilfrid Hyde White, who was a rather sophisticated light comedy actor, as the father. To see Wilfrid in boxing gloves sparring with an ex-heavyweight was hilarious. Wilfrid used to ad lib a bit: "There you are – come on fella – hey – watch it – I saw you – thought you had me that time, didn't you?"

Clearly this casting strained credulity too far and Robert Beatty took over the part. One thing I shall always remember about Wilfrid Hyde White. On the morning of the first rehearsal he arrived wearing his immaculate brown overcoat and hat. I helped him off with it when he arrived and put it on him when he left. "Very kind. Thank you so much. Very kind boy." And he put a five pound note in my hand.

Off we went on another tour where I became friends with Daniel Massey, Maureen Swanson and Leo Maguire. We went to Coventry, Manchester and Bournemouth and then came into the Cambridge Theatre to a moderate reception and a short run. My time was also up. My call-up papers came through. I wasn't altogether unhappy about it as my acting career was not exactly at a high spot, so I didn't try to fail the medical as some of my friends advised. I thought the army might make an interesting change.

My mother's sister had married a regular Coldstream Guards officer, Richard Crichton, so I applied to join that regiment and was accepted as a potential National Service officer, soon to be received unceremoniously into the Guards' depot at Caterham.

3

GUARD DUTY

I can never drive past Caterham in Surrey without a few moments of instant playback from September 1959. I must have been one of the last to be hauled into the National Service net (two years' compulsory military training upon reaching nineteen years of age). I approached the experience with an unsuspecting curiosity.

My mum and dad seemed in favour of it – I should meet a lot of interesting people, be toughened up and disciplined and have the chance to get out of show business and see what real life was about.

As a potential officer it was considered necessary for me to be treated to a brief but intense dose of private soldiery first. Colonel Erskine Crumm addressed us in one of the instruction classrooms after a formal "Sit easy!" He went on, "Remember it's tough, but so are you."

My first night in the brigade squad was traumatic. Somewhat disoriented from being screamed at by an Irish corporal, fed and watered in the Irish Guards mess hall, lectured by Trained Soldier Thorpe from Huddersfield on what would be expected of us, and unprepared for the culture shock of the NAAFI, I found that the lights were turned out about 9.30 p.m.

Dying for a smoke, I enquired in the darkness as to any possible supply, and a friendly voice to my left offered me a fag.

Having no bedroom slippers, and remembering that the floor was uncarpeted and probably full of splinters, I intended to step across from my bed to the next one in order to avoid this danger. I stepped out into the void aiming for the space at the foot of my neighbour's bed where I imagined there would be a flat landing place near to his feet.

Nothingness met my expectant downward-moving weight. The first thing that met the unfriendly floor was the tip of my nose, followed by my forehead and finally the palms of my hands. As the stars wheeled in my bruised head there was a hasty movement around me. Lights went on and Trained Soldier Thorpe came to lift me up and inspect me.

"——me!" he moaned expressively. "They'll think I stuck one on 'im." And indeed he did find it hard to convince the duty medical orderly to the contrary, but I insisted he hadn't thumped me and returned miserably to the iron bedsteads and the grinning faces of my new companions, thinking that my face might have been permanently flattened and wishing that I'd previously given up smoking.

The following morning we met Sergeant James, our platoon sergeant – short, ruddy, proud, a Welsh Guards sergeant to his blanco-less gaiter straps. I was very fond of Sergeant James – he was like a boxing glove, a slight sensation of softness but with a rock-like fist inside. Once when we were stood at ease as a brigade squad outside our hut, I imitated his Welsh accent, suggesting that he must have used a Brillo pad to make his face so shiny – a joke which he enjoyed hugely.

Our brigade officer in contrast was tall, sloping and supercilious. He arrived in a sports car from Chelsea having been groomed by his lackey, I imagined, and communicated officer class and studied non-involvement for the few brief hours he seemed to be among us. Perhaps he was the unseen hand guiding our affairs for our good. Occasionally he would accompany other officers on an amble to and fro in front of the massed company when the garrison assembled twice daily on the huge parade ground.

It was there, one afternoon, that I received a full blast of non-commissioned frenzy. Sergeant-Major Roger, Scots Guards, had assembled the massed ranks for the 2 p.m. parade. Everyone waited upon his mighty word. We were stood at ease, ready to come as one into our full uprightness at the will of the most senior officer then present. It was a sultry, hot September afternoon. Wasps droned and dived around our rigid bodies.

Suddenly one looped up underneath my friend Ingrams' forage cap and got trapped between his sticky brow and the slashed black plastic peak. In a controlled frenzy he began to direct as much air as he could upwards through his protruding lower lip, with apparently little success.

Slowly the dread giggles began to spread down the backs of the battledress jackets arrayed in the row in front of me until I too caught these infectious snorts. But needless to say, these unmilitary signals had also been communicated 150 yards to the sergeant-major's beady eye and his angry voice suddenly uttered an unrehearsed but clearly intelligible shriek.

"That guardsman, second from the left, rear rank of the brigade squad – laughing on parade. Arrest that man!"

There was a momentary search then I felt my rifle being yanked from my hand and two burly figures tucked themselves in beside me as Sergeant Jones muttered: "You dunnit this time, boy!" in my ear. Their hands grasped my elbows and lifted me two inches off the ground and like some toy soldier I was hustled off towards the guard room to the accompaniment of Sergeant-Major Roger's "Left, right, left, right, left . . ." at 120 to the minute.

At the time this did not seem like a fit punishment for what was in my view a justifiably amusing incident, but something had offended the sergeant-major, and I suppose I was spoiling his beautiful parade.

Laughing is a most wonderful experience, and the army can be credited with providing a good proportion of it in my life. What wasn't so funny was to be thumped extremely hard in the solar plexus by the surly corporal in charge of the guard-room nick upon my arrival. The opportunity to stick one on a potential officer was irresistible.

The captain was not amused either and deprived me of what little spare time I had to make me pay for my indiscretion, but I don't think I had lost favour with Sergeant Jones or Trained Soldier Thorpe when I'd finished my duties. By the end of the eight weeks' basic training they had turned us from casual young civilians into a rather sharp, spit-and-polished platoon.

Our sixteen weeks at Mons Officer Training Centre in Aldershot were designed to equip us in some of the rudiments of commanding an infantry platoon. As there were cadets from all the other infantry regiments to be trained too, we were spread through the companies, but by this time I had made good friendships with several brigade people and we tended to stick together.

At Mons I managed to do well. For some reason I was chosen by Captain Richards to lead our company in a major night exercise, but, to my shame, I cheated in the second part of our exams and so I always feel I obtained my junior under-officer's status with at least some unfair help. But I tasted just retribution a week before our passing-out parade when I could have marched before my company as their under-officer, but was felled by some powerful bug and lay in hospital for a fortnight unable to move.

Arriving at my father's flat in Old Burlington Street, London, one miserable Friday evening for a forty-eight hour leave from Mons, I found Robert Morley in the office on the floor below.

"William dear. What are you doing here?"

"I've been let off for forty-eight hours."

"How nice for you. You look very thin. Do they treat you well? Well, now, your parents have gone off to the South of France with the Sieffs. Didn't you know?"

My spirits sagged further. Dressed in my uniform with my hair clipped short and smelling somewhat of an unaired Aldershot kitbag, I was looking forward to a bit of comfort and a decent meal in familiar surroundings. Robert could see my dejection.

"Well now, what can we do?" He thought for a moment as Ros Chatto brought me in some tea and a quick fry-up of bacon and egg.

"Rossy, ring up Albany Travel and get William a plane to Nice. You'd like that. You'd like to go and see them, wouldn't you?"

I was stunned and gratefully accepted. Within minutes, Robert had effected the arrangement with gleeful aplomb and given me twenty-five pounds for the trip. By 7.30 I was dressed in civvies and on the BEA flight to the South of France. I knew they were staying in the Carlton Hotel in Cannes so when I got there I took a taxi to the hotel.

I was greeted warmly as I mentioned the Sieffs' name and was told they had all gone out to dinner at a nearby restaurant. I timidly pushed the door open and entered extremely elegant and intimate surroundings. Everyone was in evening dress and deep in conversation. The head waiter looked at me strangely, possibly catching a whiff of Mons barracks, and I peered over the tables to try and locate my parents. Suddenly I saw them sitting among about ten other diners at a long table, including Simon and Miriam Marks and Michael and Daphne Sieff. I made my way over and stood by the table. "Hello," I said.

The look of shock on their faces was not what I needed at that moment, standing exposed amidst the curious looks of the waiters and other diners.

"William," my father said, "how did you get here?"

People looked up. I felt edgy.

"Robert got me a ticket to come for the weekend. I've got forty-eight hours' leave."

Michael burst into a grin. "You great pots," he said. (Pots was his favourite term of endearment.) Then they made room for me at the table and I was ordered some *quenelles* and told by my mother to eat because I looked much too thin. I don't think they were terribly thrilled by Robert's prank but once we'd got the room sorted out I slept like a log.

My memories of the next day are of walking round the golf course with my father and the scent of the fresh mimosa which soon eased the military drudge from my mind. I returned to England the following afternoon, feeling a lot better for Robert's amazing kindness.

Upon being commissioned I received notice that I had been posted to the 3rd Battalion, Coldstream Guards, in Wellington Barracks, London. We were engaged in public duties, as was one of my best friends, Johnny Duckett. I looked forward to doing ceremonial duties in London as a fitting contrast to our recent deprivations.

Impressively attired in dark blue, three-piece pinstriped suiting with bowler hat and umbrella, I took a walk across St James's Park and up St James's Street, which I thought would be a suitable outing for my natty new accoutrements. Actually I felt like a complete twit, but was apparently accepted as normal by the unconcerned West End public, and feeling rather pleased with myself I returned to Wellington Barracks.

Being newly commissioned, tradition held that you had to be treated as if you didn't exist by other officers. You could not speak unless you were spoken to.

I was assigned a platoon which I never actually led as we were no more than well-disciplined extras in a majestic pageant. On parade we were trained and drilled endlessly to act in perfect unison, but to tell the truth I quite enjoyed the ceremonial side of life. There was something theatrical about dressing up in a red tunic, striped trousers, boots and sword belt, sash and bearskin. Our chief duties were supplying guardsmen for Trooping the Colour, mounting guard at Buckingham Palace and St James's Palace and guarding the Bank of England.

Some of my friends received invitations to parties and deb dances which took place throughout the summer. I received the occasional invitation, but I decided that this type of function was a waste of time. Others may have enthused at champagne, bacon and eggs and shifting down the Mall at four in the morning in an open sports car, but all the dawn reminded me of was the prospect of a hangover, aching feet and the difficulty of finding a taxi.

My social life was not, however, a complete blank. I was

invited by my brother Ed, who had just gone to RADA (the Royal Academy of Dramatic Art), to a drama students' party, where I met a very attractive young drama student called Sarah Miles. She was wearing a slinky dress and holding court on a sofa where she made room for me to sit down and chat. I fell for her at once. Although I must have looked rather incongruous in my pinstripe suit, socially and emotionally I felt completely at home.

Sarah had several admirers but we took up together in a very serious relationship. She spoke of the others as though they were all mad about her. Tom Courtenay and Tom Kempinski were her best friends and she was being given some of the best parts at RADA. I was even given the impression that her drama teacher was mad about her. Whether that was true or not, she was given the lead in *Six Characters in Search of an Author* and she was strikingly effective.

Sarah's dad was a steel plant designer. She was very close to her parents who accepted me as her steady and treated me with great hospitality. As they were quite well off Sarah could afford a small flat in Half Moon Street and here we began what was for both of us our first real intimate relationship. It was just a short walk across the park from Wellington Barracks and I made the trip often.

However, the army was about to halt our short-lived bliss. I was posted to Kenya with the 2nd Battalion when the 3rd Battalion was disbanded. The last ten months of my National Service stretched before me like an eternity, separated from Sarah.

I arrived out in Kenya just before Christmas and found that I knew one other officer in the regiment, Peter Ingrams, with whom I had been at Caterham. The 2nd Battalion were camped at Gilgil, in the Rift Valley, just off the main road from Nakuru to Nairobi, seventy miles away.

The living accommodation was entirely tented. The officers' and sergeants' messes and guard room were a little more solid. The battalion had been in Kenya as part of the 24th Brigade for about six months. I believe our role was to protect Britain's oil interests and to be a 'presence' in pre-independence Kenya.

There was a friendly spirit in the battalion. The officers' mess, which had a dining room attached, was the main meeting place. In the entrance hall hung a mail rack, the focus of attention for me. Sarah was an affectionate, faithful and funny correspondent, and her letters were my most prized possession.

I shared a tent with Ingrams. It was about twenty by fifteen feet, with enough room to stand in. There we slept, or lay on our beds listening to Peter's gramophone records. Another officers' tent, number twelve, belonged to Sam Barnett and Tim Tollemache. The most usual diversion after getting pestilentially drunk in the mess was to retire there to play our favourite record of Noël Coward in Las Vegas.

I gave quite a passable imitation of Noël singing Señorita Nina from Argentina, and also Poor Uncle Harry who wanted to be a missionary, but my abiding memory is lurching round one of the large tent poles in a kind of reel, shouting the song from *High Society*: "Well did you ever . . . what a swelegant, elegant party this is!"

The emphasis in Kenya was slightly more military than in London. I was given a platoon to command in No. 2 Company with Sergeant Pickles. Our company commander was Mike Mitchell, an extremely friendly and popular person. Exercises were organised at regular intervals and we shared one exercise with No. 1 Company. This was commanded by Major Peter Hills, who had a very enthusiastic spirit. His junior officers, Sam Barnett, Tom Tollemache and Simon Forster, would manage to organise a party even on an exercise in the desert.

Our adjutant, David Middleton, a keen horseman, helped me to get started as a polo player. I was mounted on some rusty old charger and given one or two practice knock-abouts with the battalion team who played a local side on Sunday mornings. Our opponents included the well-known Digby Thatham-Water, who was famous for his exploits at

Arnhem with his umbrella, which he put up when the shelling was heavy; he was one of the few parachutists to survive the battle.

The largest exercise we took part in involved airlifting the brigade to Aden and holding the surrounding desert in the event of an attempted enemy takeover. I'm glad it wasn't the real thing, because – as I recall – half the battalion's signals equipment had to be jettisoned from the Beverley transporter over the Gulf of Aden to keep the aircraft stable after three of its four engines had conked out.

On our arrival it was so hot that no one could do much moving about during the day, and we gobbled salt tablets, which were supposed to keep us upright. One day I received a telegram in my forward dug-out position. It read: "Congratulations on your majority. Love, Pa." It had arrived on my twenty-first birthday.

At night I and my platoon crept forth on a patrol but unfortunately we failed to find the enemy position. We returned with little to report. Warfare can be a hit and miss affair.

On our return we were happy to exchange the salt tablets for large gins and tonics at the Muthaiga Club. From time to time we could get a few days' leave in Nairobi, Mombasa and Malindi. My first visit to the beautiful east coast of Kenya was memorable. I travelled with Robin Shuldham and Jonathan van der Werff in Robin's VW, and reaching Mombasa at about 4 p.m. we decided to press on that evening up the coast the seventy-odd miles to Malindi.

The road became increasingly narrow, rutted and sandy, and we craned forward to try and spot the deep holes in the *murram* early enough to dodge round them. The journey was taking a lot longer than we expected and at about midnight, feeling peckish and fed up with careering along what looked like a farm track through a palm forest, we suddenly dipped and scraped into a large crater where we came to a stop. The engine died. We tried it for about half an hour, until the battery was only feebly coughing, and then gave up. We discussed the situation, and the two captains decided that since we were about fifteen miles from Malindi, they would walk to the hotel and send back a towing vehicle as soon as they could, while I should stay and guard the car.

I rather hesitantly agreed to this plan. Moving to the front seat, I watched them marching purposefully down the moonlit track. Alone in the stranded VW, my imagination was racing with horrible thoughts of Mau Mau headhunters and slimy cobras. I've never looked for the sunrise with more expectancy.

When it came I reckoned Robin and Jonathan should just about be arriving in Malindi, so with luck they should be back in a couple of hours. I tried the ignition key for luck and the car purred into life. At once relief flooded in. I slipped the car into first, eased it out of the pit and was off and chugging down the road. A steady drizzle had begun. After travelling a few miles, I saw two familiar figures in the middle of the road. I lowered my window and asked if I could give them a lift, and we nosed on towards our destination, tired, relieved and ready for a holiday.

Our adventures in the VW were not over, though. One day we set off for a nearby beach for a picnic, and chose a spot close to the coastal road we had travelled up a few days before. We decided to take the car on to the beach, confident that the sand was firm, especially close to the water, where the tide had impacted it hard.

We got on to the beach all right and chugged to the tidal edge of the sand, intending to press on a little farther to choose a nice spot. But hardly had we gone a few yards before the body began sinking and we heard the sand scraping along its underside. Desperately we tried to head for higher, firmer ground, but the more we tried the farther we sank into the sand.

Out we jumped and started to push, but the back wheels dug in still farther. At the same time we felt our shoes filling up with water as the sea slid into the deep ruts where the wheels were embedded. Hurriedly we shoved anything we could lay our hands on under the wheels to give them something to bite on. We heaved some more; a heavier surge of water engulfed the car and we were up to our ankles in shifting sand.

It was clear we weren't going to move the VW and that the incoming tide was going to win the battle. Reluctantly we started to move off up the beach to watch the fate of the poor car. Jonathan had left the engine on and I was surprised how long it went on puttering as the water rose above the exhausts at the back – a tribute to German engineering, I thought. But finally she lay awash in the surf with three downcast spectators watching aghast.

My salary as an officer was 28s 6d a week, which didn't go very far. One incident put a major strain on my finances. It had to do with a car again. Mike Panter from the 3rd Battalion had driven out to Kenya from England with a couple of friends in a long-wheelbased Land-Rover. It was a good effort as they had negotiated the Sahara and survived a number of adventures with the Bedouin.

Mike was second in command of our company, which was engaged in an exercise up in the north of Kenya on the farmland of the Duke of Manchester. The Duke asked us for a drink and in true Kenya fashion everyone was well oiled by the time we came to leave. I offered to drive the Land-Rover with Mike and Kevin Fellowes, the adjutant. We wound our way down from the Duke's hilltop house all right, but as we picked up speed on the plain I was caught out by a deceptively sharp bend, left the road and hit a tree very hard.

Mike banged his knee. I was all right but the chassis had been shoved back eight inches and the bill was about £200 which Mike passed on to me.

When my time as a National Service officer came to an end, Peter Ingrams and I flew back to England, but not before I had considered extending my service for three more years. For the army's sake I'm glad I didn't, but the thoughts of acting had receded amid the diversions of military life, and my main motive for returning to England was to be back with Sarah and to earn some money to pay for the damage to the Land-Rover.

4

TERM OF TRIAL – THE SERVANT

On my return to England I was struck by the cramped rows of neat suburban semis that contrasted so much with the sparsely inhabited Kenyan bush, heavy with heat, roaming cattle and noble Masai herdsmen, and broken by the pink shimmer of the flamingo-trimmed waters of Lake Nakuru.

Life was going to be different, as I immediately learned from my dad. He offered me a bed in his Old Burlington Street flat, but suggested I get a job right away to support myself and pay off my debt.

It was only a quarter of a mile from my father's flat to Fortnum and Mason in Piccadilly, so I wandered down there in search of a job and was taken on as a temporary on the biscuit counter. The senior staff – Mr Lunn, Mr Hobbs and Mr Barratt – served the great and small with equal courtesy, but they did manage to serve a few more of the great than we temporaries. It was a rare excitement when we got an order of over fifty pounds.

The previous two years had separated me from the actor's life and I wondered if I wanted to continue in the profession. My homecoming to Sarah was not an unmixed blessing. She had been taken up by a much older friend of mine and, though she said she wanted to continue with me, there were traumas for all of us. She had moved to a flat in Judd Street, St Pancras, which she shared with a girlfriend named Hattie Critall. The hit record of the time was 'Milor' by Edith Piaf. I felt like the Milor that Piaf seemed to mock in her song and its whirling and accelerating frenzies seemed to catch us all in their spell. Nevertheless, Sarah and I began again, and our relationship seemed at times to be better than ever. At weekends we drove to the Miles' family home at Ingatestone and played tennis and croquet.

On Christmas Eve the Fortnum's staff all dug a table-spoon into a huge can of Beluga caviar. We crammed the melting salty deliciousness into our mouths as a tasty toast to our rich customers.

But serving at Fortnum's was only a stop-gap. I had to move on. But where to? I thought I wanted a more secure and respectable job but one where I could be creative. I hit on the idea of becoming an advertising executive.

My parents, through their friendship with the Sieff family, helped to get me introduced to Saward Baker who handled the Marks and Spencer account, and they accepted me. I became an assistant account executive.

As well as Marks and Spencer, my bosses' main clients were Maenson suits and the International Wool Secretariat. The work entailed submitting artwork and copy to the clients for their approval and placing ads in the provincial papers. For the International Wool we made a five-minute colour film for presentation in about 450 cinemas. I really had nothing to offer creatively and although I was grateful for the work I realised after a year that I was not motivated by anything to do with advertising.

About Christmas time I heard that Tony Richardson was looking for a public-school type for a small part in *The Loneliness of the Long Distance Runner*. I went to see him on location in Hammersmith. He told me what was in-volved and that the part was that of the best public-school runner in the race against the Borstal where the hero, Tom Courtenay, was a pupil. The public-school boy won the race when Tom refused to cross the finishing line, even though he got there first.

He told me it would take four days and I would get £120. I had to decide whether to take this part or stay in advertis-ing after Christmas, and without much difficulty I took it.

Richardson, who had directed the original production of *Look Back in Anger* at the Royal Court, had just made a film, *A Taste of Honey*, with an unknown actress in the lead,

Rita Tushingham. He didn't use the studio but set his camera up in an old institution for my one scene in the runners' dressing room and in a field and on the back of a car for the running sequences. He was married to Vanessa Redgrave at the time. She came to be with us, standing in the crowd with the extras cheering the race.

Tom Courtenay was making his first film. He had been cast for his brilliant acting and extraordinary gaunt looks. I had met him briefly at the RADA, through Sarah. He knew exactly how it felt for me to be playing a small part and for him to be the star. He joked a lot about being 'the star' and sent himself up, but I respected him because he shared his pleasure in the breaks he was getting and took his job seriously without being ponderous about it. He had to run a lot farther than I did but Richardson nearly killed me chasing him in the camera car.

When the film was over I unhesitatingly quit advertising even though I had only £120 in the bank and no prospects. I knew this was where I fitted and I was beginning to circulate with people in the business again through my family and Sarah. At this time I began to believe I could succeed as an actor and the taste of working for Richardson and the new wave made me excited about the talent that was emerging in British films.

This time my father offered to become my agent again. It was a happy arrangement as we got on extremely well and I had great respect for him as an agent. During his time in management with Robert Morley they had produced several hits including *For Adults Only*, *Tunnel of Love* and *The Rape of the Belt*, but they had also had a few expensive misses. The third member of the management was Ros Chatto who now became a partner.

Having done these plays my father decided to get back to what he was best at, representing actors and directors. The only things he would ever divulge about his clients or friends were in hilarious imitations. He did 'Binkie' Beaumont and Jimmy Woolf – two of his close friends – brilliantly. His advice to me was "work with good directors" and he always said "Let's read the script". He kept his love of the theatre alive by serving on the Royal Court Theatre Board and the Arts Council. His friends and client list was like *Who's Who in the Theatre*: Lindsay Anderson, John Osborne, Joe Losey, Vanessa Redgrave, Tony Richardson, Paul Scofield, Robert Morley and others. He soon snatched up Sarah Miles, as he also came under her charm. She used to bring her enormous Pyrenean mountain dog into his rather grand office and get away with it. In fact, she had him eating out of her hand.

My father had a unique telephone manner. He would cradle the receiver on his shoulder and gaze wistfully, or he would bow his head with it between his knees or he would throw his head back with groans of amusement. He was a tremendous audience and to those of us who sat waiting for his attention, listening to these one-sided conversations, he was also a great performer. My mother always said that he was a disappointed actor.

Dad sent Sarah off to Worthing to get some experience on the stage after RADA. I followed her. She played in two or three plays and again I knew that she was making the actors she played with fall in love with her and I started to become jealous. I spent almost all my time in the theatre or driving her to a friend of her parents at Brighton or to my mother's home which she used as digs. She had to stay up late and learn her lines and I used to hear them. But it was worth it. I was in love.

Sarah was then cast in H. M. Tennent's production of *Dazzling Prospect* with Margaret Rutherford. The play toured in Dublin before coming to The Globe. In Dublin our relationship reached a height of passion; we only left the hotel to go to the theatre. The play was not a huge success but Sarah was written about and photographed everywhere. She always had a good quote for the press and looked amusing as well as pretty, pulling Addo, her Pyrenean mountain dog, around with her wherever she went. By being original and genuine she got more attention than the pin-up starlets, but she was quite jealous of her rivals.

Full of confidence, she tested for Peter Glenville's *Term of Trial* and was offered the part of the fifteen-year-old school-girl who gets a crush on her middle-aged schoolteacher. On a trip to Paris, she forces herself on him, but is gently rebuffed, and as a punishment tries to discredit him in a scandal.

For the part of the schoolmaster, Jimmy Woolf, the producer, engaged Laurence Olivier, and the part of the classroom Casanova was played by Terry Stamp. Filming was in Ardmore Studios near Dublin, and I went over there whenever I could.

Like every actor I was deeply in awe of Sir Laurence. Sarah was not only in awe, but in love. He was remarkably friendly and gentle, expressing the retiring characteristics of his current part rather than the expected qualities of roman-tic, kingly presence. Terry had just burst on to the scene with his performance as Billy Budd in Peter Ustinov's film, and I both admired and was extremely jealous of him. He was one of the first to change the image of the young actor; working class, ambitious, irreverent, funny and pert.

The film launched Sarah into star status but she chose to follow it up with Laurence Harvey's directorial debut, *The Ceremony*, which was made in Madrid. I dutifully followed her there, too, but it was a comedown for Sarah when the film flopped.

At this time I got another film part, this time in Philip Leacock's *Tahamine*. I played a schoolboy – not a very memorable experience, except for the opportunity to admire Derek Nimmo's comedy of breathless embarrassment as a public-school master, bowled over by an Eastern beauty, Nancy Kwan. But it *was* work and it led to something better.

Anglia TV produced plays regularly for ITV and George More O'Farrall was to direct one called *The Door*, about an older woman's friendship and influence upon a young man. I was cast in my first leading role and it was also my first experience of television. On transmission we ran the play through right from beginning to end, unlike today, when it is pre-recorded, chopped up and then edited together. Ann Todd and I really hit it off and something exciting came across.

I was still looking for the right name as an actor at that time. In *The Door* I was Oliver Fox but it didn't seem right. Sarah and I were asked to the first night of Jimmy Woolf's production of Bryan Forbes' film *The L-Shaped Room*. We were feeling and looking pretty good, and, turning round in our stall seats, who should we see but Dirk Bogarde who acknowledged us. We waved back, then turned to one another, highly flattered. After the film there was a premiere party and we were placed on a table with Dirk's friend and manager Tony Forwood.

"What do you think of *The Servant* then?" he said to Sarah.

"Why?" stalled Sarah.

"Because Dirk wants to do it and he wants you for Vera."

"Me?" squeaked Sarah. "Oh . . . no . . ."

She acted mock modesty.

"Yes, and wouldn't your friend be good as Tony?"

"Willy. Y-e-s, wouldn't he."

She was thinking fast but the action seemed to be going faster. I was introduced to Tony.

"I know your father — come and see us at the Connaught tomorrow for a drink before lunch, at about 12.30 — you too." He looked directly at me. "Dirk would like to meet you and he would like you to meet Joe as well."

The conversation quickly got back to how wonderful *The L-Shaped Room* had been but our minds were on what had just happened. A big star had just passed a message that he wanted to do a picture because of Sarah and there might be a part for *me*!! This was a night to remember.

We got up early the following day and made ready to meet Dirk for drinks before lunch. Sarah, for once, left Addo behind and we got to the Connaught and left her white Mini to collect its customary two-pound parking fine. Well groomed hotel staff eyed us as if knowing we were expected and showed us to the lift and asked, "Mr

Bogarde's suite?" Up to the third floor and out into the quiet corridor, a knock on the door, and it was Dirk himself.

"Hello – lovely to see you – what did you think of the party? Tote told me he met you both." Dirk was in an elegant grey suit with casual black moccasins from Gucci, with a Guinness and a Kent cigarette on the go.

"What d'you want to drink?"

"Vodka and tonic," said Sarah.

"I'll have the same."

"What about a champagne cocktail?" said Dirk. "Much nicer."

It was sent for. We relaxed in the comfortable armchairs. Joe Losey arrived shortly afterwards and was grumpy.

He acknowledged us. "Hello." His voice lifted a bit as he shook hands with Sarah. As we shook hands, he looked at me quite hard. Then he turned away shyly and nervously, but his mood had changed a bit. "Yes, I'll have a vodka – do you mind if I open a window?"

Joe was fiftyish and American, with the appearance of an asthmatic intellectual Red Indian Chief without the feathers. He rumbled on about things that had gone wrong that day and other bad news: one of his films had been massacred in an unauthorised cut version and he intended to sue the company. He wolfed his vodka, and Dirk, who seemed to know his guest, filled him up again.

"We-e-ell," he moaned, "what about you two?" Then he went off again on another story of woe, this time to do with someone who was letting him down over *The Servant*. "Have you read it?"

No we hadn't.

"I'll get a script for you." He rang his secretary. "Get a script to Sarah and er – what's your name?"

"Will," said Dirk.

"And one for Willie," said Joe, deliberately sounding the 'ie'. (Sarah called me Willie.) "We still haven't got the money."

Dirk spoke to me. "I saw you in *The Door* by chance and thought you were very good."

"What's that?" said Joe, not liking having missed the reference.

"*The Door* on television, a play with Ann Todd."

"Oh," said Joe, bored.

"If we don't do it now, everyone will be unavailable."

The interview went on a bit longer, Sarah charming Tony and Dirk, Joe still looking gloomy. We felt it was time to go.

"You'll get the scripts later today," he promised.

Dirk showed us to the door. "I think you'll be marvellous for it," he said to Sarah as we left. "It's a terrific risk for all of us but we've got to do it."

Later that day our scripts came. It was a Friday evening and we were due to go to Cuckfield. Sarah's way of reading a script was to roll the pages through beneath her thumb to check how often her character's name was mentioned. "I don't think I like this," she said, sitting on the bed. By her evaluation the part of Tony came off much better, because his name appeared on every page. I read it avidly. It was not only the quantity but the quality of the part that I could see. It was quite a short script but a really good read. I finished it and thought 'wow'.

"What do you think?" said Sarah.

"Wonderful. What about you?"

"It's a marvellous part for you."

"*And* you," I said, meaning it.

The story-line was unusual and arresting. Tony, a wealthy young aristocrat, sets himself up in a Chelsea house and needs someone to run it for him. He is engaged to Susan (Wendy Craig) and dabbles in business. Barrett applies for the job and impresses Tony with his ideas ("simple and classical is best, I always think, sir"). He gets the job — plans the menus, runs the bar, arranges the flowers and upsets the fiancée. Tony is rather protective.

"I think we need a girl, sir, to help in the house."

"Girl, what sort of girl?" Tony asks.

"A maid."

"Oh, do you?"

"Yes, sir, they can be very useful."

Vera is introduced as Barrett's sister. Unsisterly goings-on occur in the top-floor bedroom. One night Vera offers herself to Tony, hoisting herself up on the kitchen table. Tony is hooked on Vera. But, coming back early one weekend, Tony and Susan find Barrett and Vera together in Tony's bed. He throws them both out of the house.

However, Tony can't manage on his own. Barrett returns to say sorry, and Tony has him back. Barrett gets Vera back and plays hide-and-seek and ball games on the stairs with Tony. Barrett invites other friends to the house, and then introduces Tony to a potion from a gentleman in Jermyn Street. Tony becomes zombie-like. Barrett promises to mend his ways but is now more dominant than Tony. The end! Harold Pinter had created a riveting drama.

Joe rang on Sunday. "What do you think?"

My father had now read it and, though he had reservations about my ability to do it, he thought it was very effective and contained a good part for Sarah. I had no doubts and told him so.

"I'll have to do a screen test on you."

He wanted to see if I could manage the last scenes where Tony is on drugs, so he hired a studio and crew and set me up with half a tumbler of brandy, let it work, and then told me to say some of the lines to him standing by the camera. He topped up my glass every now and then and, apparently satisfied, got me back to his flat in London to sober up. He paid for the test out of his own pocket.

The next thing, having found their Tony, was to find the money. No one was really interested to back the film – I think the budget was about £120,000 – but everyone connected with it was prepared to take cuts in their salaries to get it off the ground. Eventually my father persuaded Leslie Grade to put up the last of the money.

Finally I had to decide on a name for myself.

One weekend I was staying at my parents' and Ros Chatto and Tom, her husband, and their two sons James and Daniel, were staying there as well. Jamie and Danny slept in the room next to mine and as I was wrestling with my name problem in the early hours of the morning, James crept through my bedroom to go to the loo. As he did so, I thought 'James is a nice name . . .' and decided to adopt it, with his approval.

Next Joe had a really wonderful idea to help me with my approach to filming. He proposed that I work for two weeks prior to shooting with an actor/director he knew called Vivian Matalon. I went to Viv's flat in West London rather nervously. He was about thirty-five, American and serious, but I liked him right away. He seemed to admire the script and was extremely interesting about it. He wanted to coach me so that I would be prepared and confident before we got to the camera. He introduced me to a rewarding system of approaching a part.

Even though the character I was playing, Tony, was close to my own experience and temperament I still needed to understand how to communicate that. We worked on simple intentions for each scene. Some were easier than others but in Harold Pinter's dialogue there is room for the sub-text and interior dialogue to be developed, and it was important to discover these layers.

The interview with Barrett was the first and hardest scene. It was virtually a monologue for me. Here it was essential that I could move and say the lines comfortably, telling Barrett what his job entailed.

We explored my attitude towards the other characters. Tony really thinks of Barrett as a fussy old maid, but he feels that one has to put up with one's servants.

Tony's feelings for Susan are mixed. He likes her physically but wants her to like Barrett too. Vera awakens unexpressed desires and exposes chinks in Tony's suavity.

Another scene I found hard was the ball game on the stairs. We decided that the solution was to play it as if I really wanted to win and enjoyed poking fun at Barrett's poor gamesmanship. The hide-and-seek scene evolved through discussing it and trying different approaches. Many people have found this one of the most effective scenes in the film. The way into it for me was simply to remember what it was like to play hide-and-seek when I was seven or eight.

For the drug scenes at the end Joe had some ghastly glycerine drops put in my eyes to make them blurred and watery. He also decided that I needed to bleach my hair and 'Bumble' Dawson supplied some nice clothes.

We shot nearly all of it in Shepperton Studios within ten weeks, even though Joe had to be off the film for a week with pneumonia. His direction was meticulous in every detail.

I only appreciated it fully when I saw what he had created on the screen. It was hard to recognise anything of Dirk's natural self in the malevolent character he was playing. We became good friends and sat drinking coffee and chatting for hours in his caravan on the set. Obviously we had a close working relationship for the film, but our friendship went beyond that. I became a frequent visitor on Sundays to his house near Guildford. He enjoyed a lot of things I liked – his home, walking with the dogs, talking about the business and the garden and country life, about which he was very knowledgeable. He had an attractive circle of friends, like John and Jill Standing, and Noel and Sarah Harrison.

At the same time we never talked directly about our roles or what we were doing in the film. We just let what had been soaked into us about our parts come out on the set. Joe's direction and the script made it work.

On the last day of the film we were in a pub in Chelsea when suddenly I got in an awful panic. I thought, will I ever be able to act again? Or is this a one-off thing? I felt with a cold shock that I'd lost all my own talent. I rang Dirk. He was quite used to end of picture let-downs and told me how hard he was finding it to take off Barrett's clothes and put them back in the trunk. We both had a difficult time for a while, waiting for the film to be released.

Finally, the film was to open. I had invited Jackie Lane to the premiere – Sarah was Terry Stamp's guest. The cracks were growing larger in our relationship. But all we could think of that night and the following day was the brilliant reception the press gave to *The Servant*.

5

TYPECAST

One of the results of the overnight·success of *The Servant* was that it fixed me very firmly in the minds of film makers and journalists as the decadent upper-class type.

Peter Evans, the writer, suggested I get an E-Type Jaguar and date some of the beautiful starlets to make an impression around London and establish my image. I had been able to convey an air of class and wealth in *The Servant* and it seemed that I would be strongly considered for any similar parts that were offered.

Twentieth Century-Fox planned some major European productions in the summer of 1964; one was *The Sound of Music*. The other, in which I was offered a good part, was *Those Magnificent Men in Their Flying Machines*.

Sarah Miles played the beautiful young daughter of newspaper-owning, race-sponsoring Robert Morley, and I was to be the young British Guards officer-aviator engaged to Sarah – so it was a bit of a family affair. Having stars like Gert Frobe, Stuart Whitman, Jean Pierre Cassel and Alberto Sordi in the picture led Robert Morley to ad lib in one scene: "The trouble with these international events is that they attract so many foreigners!"

The stars of the film, however, were the machines themselves, which behaved beautifully in the glorious hot summer while we filmed at Booker Aerodrome near High Wycombe. I never actually flew my plane but I did taxi it along the ground, and 'took it up' in the studio with blue-screen back projection, and on the side of a hill in a mock-up which travelled along rails and could tip and bank.

As in *The Loneliness of the Long Distance Runner*, I achieved a hollow victory in this film. The leader in the race, the American Stuart Whitman, sacrifices his first place to rescue Alberto Sordi, whose plane is on fire. I also had to 'lose the girl' at the end of the picture, when she chose the handsome Stu instead of me.

Art mirrored reality in this instance, as I was about to lose Sarah. There was a bitter end to our relationship. We had not been getting along too well during the filming and when it was over she went almost immediately into a Henry Livings play, *Kelly's Eye*, at the Royal Court, in which she played opposite Nicol Williamson and became attracted to him.

Nicol was an actor I admired tremendously. He had been a close friend of my brother Ed while they were at Dundee Rep. But as a rival he was altogether too overpowering. I remember being assaulted by his verbals, humiliated in the Royal Court pub, and forced to slink away defeated.

I ran to my mother, who was a great comfort and assured me that time 'heals everything'. But I remember thinking how unconsoling that advice is in the painful moment of separating. At least the separation was abrupt and final.

While I was recovering I went out with beautiful Jackie Lane and appeared in a musical version of *The Rivals*. Both experiences were fast, fun and not for very long. Then by good chance I was offered not only a serious and good part, but an opportunity to work in Hollywood.

King Rat was a James Woolf production of James Clavell's prisoner-of-war story. The director was Bryan Forbes, whose films *The Angry Silence*, *The L-Shaped Room* and *Whistle Down the Wind* I had loved. It was a wonderful follow-up to *The Servant*.

King Rat is the story of an American corporal in Changi Jail in 1945, who not only survives but thrives in the camp by operating a black market in cigarettes, booze and drugs for both prisoners and guards. In his dealings he uses a young RAF officer, Peter Marlowe, as an interpreter. That was the part I played. It was modelled on the author James

An Actor's Entrance
Above left: Even in his pram James charms before the camera.
Above right: James holds baby Robert with Edward standing
alongside. *Below:* Like father, like son: Robin and James Fox in
characteristic pose.

Child Star
With Greer Garson and Walter Pidgeon in *The Miniver Story* and
(below) as the young Liverpool hero of *The Magnet*.

Developing Image
Above left: Shortly after leaving Harrow. *Above right and below:*
The young star through the sixties.

Off and Running
Passing a shattered Tom Courtenay in *Loneliness of the Long Distance Runner*, and (below) hospitalised in *King Rat*.

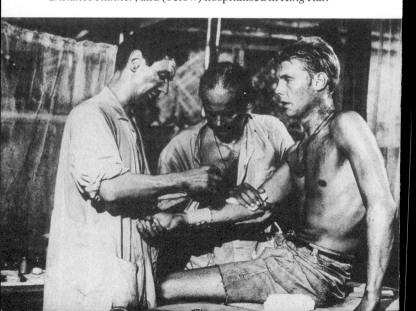

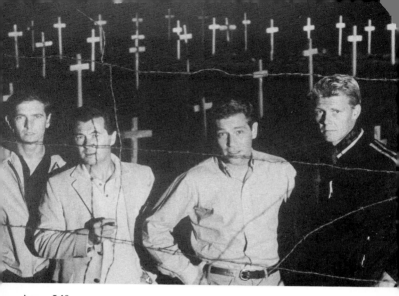

Army Life
Above: Barbed Quartet: James with Tom Courtenay, Bryan Forbes and George Segal on location for *King Rat. Below:* Young Adventurer: with the Guards in Kenya astride an MGA.

The Servant
With director Joseph Losey in the role that established his image
alongside the man who turned him from the dominant (above) to
the docile (below) – Dirk Bogarde.

A Taste of Tapioca
Dancing with Julie Andrews in *Thoroughly Modern Millie*.

Assorted Company
Above: With co-star James Coburn at a party for *Thoroughly Modern Millie. Below left:* With Vanessa Redgrave in a scene from *Isadora. Below right:* A view from the raft behind the Indian guide on his Amazon odyssey.

Clavell's own experiences. I looked forward to playing the part of a man who had survived by courage, wit and real friendship.

Bryan Forbes wrote as well as directed, and I responded to his sympathy. We all went on a strict diet to get to the necessary skinniness and ate our raw carrot lunches together throughout the production. These ardours were relieved by the great atmosphere of laughter and comradeship which Bryan created. It spilled over into the film, giving the characters the kind of qualities which make survival possible, even in Changi.

Jimmy Woolf, the producer, had brought to the Coast a whole coachload of good British prisoner-of-war types – John Mills, Alan Webb (who already lived in the US), Denholm Elliott, Leonard Rossiter, Gerald Sim, James Donald, Tom Courtenay and John Standing. Most of us were new to Hollywood but Hollywood seemed unruffled by this strange emaciated British troupe, presumably having been invaded all its life by intrepid fortune hunters from distant shores.

Armed with my expenses of an undreamed-of 250 dollars a week, I got myself unpacked in the Chateau Marmont Hotel, having swiftly moved out of the Sunset Something which was too tacky.

Jimmy and Bryan helped us acclimatise in their delightful rented villas situated several hundred feet above the busy Sunset Boulevard in Beverly Hills. Los Angeles was not quite what I expected – where was Hollywood? And the answer, when I went touring the next day, was appropriately: nowhere exactly.

But to go anywhere, I was informed, you had to have a car, and so the first priority was to hire my first American auto. It was a huge thing with a front seat that extended right across and you could turn the wheel with your index finger. Immediately I got into it I coveted the next American car I saw, which had a roof which was, at that very moment, opening electrically with a buzzing sound to expose its decorative driver.

This seemed to me to be Hollywood culture in a capsule — what you have may be nice, but it's not as nice as what you could have.

My excitement having been modulated I got back to appreciating my own vehicle. First, it had been so simple to get: a call to a friendly rental company and ten minutes later, with the exchange of some of my expenses . . . the keys . . . the ramp . . . the sunlight . . . and the Strip!

Next, the radio: KRLA. What a wonder! This was 1964 and my previous listening to commercial radio had been Radio Lux under the blankets after lights out at Harrow. I was hooked on American airwaves at the push of a button. A brash and continuous flow of music and ads encased me and I became captive to the prevailing mood and system of day-to-day LA.

It was beguiling and fascinating. Even the weather and smog reports were works of pop salesmanship — the announcer gave the news of the weather due importance: "Today there is a high of 82 in Redondo Beach, Garden City and Sausolito, with a low tonight of 62, slight hill fog in the San Fernando Valley. The smog count an average 2.4, the weatherman says it will continue dry, warm and sunny, you're tuned to KRLA." You believed him, because it was and it would be. This was Happy Town, USA!

The freeways, or motorways, gave me another view of American attitudes. Lane discipline is strictly observed: you choose one of four speeds you want to go. Speed is something everyone has, so nobody is trying to outpedal the other man. Superiority is expressed in newness (rapidity of turnover). Besides, freeways were patrolled by heavies on Harley-Davidsons called the Highway Patrol, whose job was to terrify the would-be transgressor into freeway conformity.

The war in Vietnam was the main news item. Every day on the radio, on the hour, every hour, there were two minutes of the world's miseries, rendered innocuous by the media's presentation.

The raids into North Vietnam were also dealt with like a

commercial slot; the hundreds of war protesters marching were all grist to the mill for ol' KRLA.

Hollywood to me wasn't a place – it was a way of thinking. I let it enfold me and draw me into its fantasy. What did Hollywood want to do with me? I don't think they were quite sure. One of the best agents in town, Gerry Terkofsky, who was masterminding George Segal's career, was full of ideas for Tom Courtenay and myself, but I was not represented by William Morris, his agency, so he couldn't hustle for me.

Tom would tell me about the interest he was getting from one of the big independent producers for an epic in Hawaii and my agent Sol would tell me I was going to be invited by the same company to be in one of their productions. The money discussed was of the six figure variety and yet the projects had a way of being full of promise, but slow to be fulfilled.

Hollywood is the city of deals; I was an unknown commercial ásset. As Brits we had to play cool and get on with our picture while we learnt the language and savoured the scene.

Tom fulfilled one of his fantasies by dating the beautiful Natalie Wood. We teased him about it, but, like a true gentleman, he took it pretty seriously. His other interest was golf, which appeared to be the movie industry's number one sport.

Mike Frankovich, the head of Columbia Pictures (the studio that was making *King Rat*), was an ex-football player and kindly took me to a couple of games in which UCLA, the local university side, were playing. I could understand the purpose but not the strategy, which required a certain insight into how and who is travelling ten yards with the ball before being mown down by a marauding horde of armour-clad giants. It was an effective display of macho manliness which appeared to be hugely enjoyed by the crowd.

My mother and father came out to stay with Jimmy and see me, and the very American-ness of LA made my father become more English. He brought his umbrella with him, although it hardly ever rains, and he would actually go for *walks* from Jimmy's house, which was a near impossible thing to do as there are no pavements in Beverly Hills and no provision for the walker.

As this activity proved to be dangerous we came to rely instead on bathing in Jimmy's swimming pool, which at the time had its heating system out of action. When Jimmy's black manservant saw my mother enjoying a dip in a pleasant seventy-five degrees or so, he exclaimed: "Oh, Mrs Fox! You're too much!" and went inside to tell of the English eccentricities to the cook.

Jimmy was a droll and naughty but hugely enjoyable host. The then current favourite drink was a Bull-Shot (vodka and cold consommé) and Jimmy, eager to make the party go and loosen people up, had Ireland, his chauffeur, mix drinks of massive alcoholic proportions for some of his guests. Famous starlets swooned and Jimmy would pronounce with mock disapproval how badly their mothers had brought them up, and we all fell about with laughter.

Jimmy's favourite, Laurence Harvey, was known by him at this time as 'Centre-piece' because of his insistence on always being positioned stage centre in every scene in which he appeared in *Camelot* at Drury Lane.

"Centre-piece will be deeply offended if he's offered a penny less than 125,000 dollars for his performance," he would relate with amusement. "You'd think the figure had been settled by an act of Congress."

The shooting of the film went well, and we got on splendidly with George Segal – who played the corporal – Pat O'Neal and the other American actors. I think George is an engaging actor, self-mocking in a Jewish way.

As Marlowe, I had to learn a short speech in Malayan to impress him with my usefulness as a translator. On the rehearsals I got it right and George's mouth dropped open.

"Veerry good. How about that, Bryan? Did you write that? You did that very well, Fox!"

"We'll have to give Mother Seagull a large extra close-up

for her reaction shot or she'll be mortally offended about being left with egg on her face," said Bryan consolingly.

"I will, I will, you're right. What is this with you English, who is this movie all about anyway?" There was continuous banter.

The scenes I remember most vividly are the harrowing ones where I get gangrene and face amputation of my arm. In one scene I'm asked to join in a four at bridge with two other officers and a padre. He jokingly refers to my bid saying, "You ought to have more faith, Pete."

I flare up. "Faith, is that what you said? Is that what you're talking about – faith – God – that sort of thing? Do you think God can do anything, really do anything, I mean?"

The padre replies, "He can heal."

"Heal – do what? Heal! vicar, padre or whatever you call yourself – well he's done a pretty good job here, hasn't he? This is one of his major successes. People dying of dysentery and starvation. Don't talk to me about God – you know what you can do with your precious God, vicar? You can work it."

This outburst as Marlowe faces his terrible predicament was difficult to act because it had to be sustained and felt. I wasn't an atheist at the time but I could feel for Marlowe, lashing out at what he saw was the apparent indifference and powerlessness of a supposedly loving and all-powerful creator. Only later did I come to discover that God has not remained indifferent to human suffering, nor has he left us alone.

Bryan and Jimmy felt we'd got a really good film, and Columbia, who were brave enough to let Bryan have artistic freedom, had made a very English production in Hollywood. James Clavell, who wrote it, was to my thinking the forerunner of a new breed, the English expatriate successfully selling his Englishness in a world market.

Another rather better known example, the Beatles, made their first West Coast appearance while I was in Los Angeles. The culture barrier was being breached by a different Englishness, one that was in high contrast to the stiff upper lip quality of our film.

The Beatles were being heavily promoted on my radio station and when they went to the baseball stadium I crammed in, along with 65,000 others. That experience was a disappointment because of the poor amplification and visibility, but the impression remained of a new society to which I felt drawn – international, unfettered – and rocking.

6

HOLLYWOOD

I left LA ten days before Christmas – my destination, New York. I wanted to see it, stay over Christmas with a girl-friend and see Dirk Bogarde and Tony Forwood, who were doing Christmas 1964, New York style.

Icy draughts racing round Manhattan's street corners acted like adrenalin. Inside the buildings, you cooked. Dehydration on top of jet lag caused a thirst problem, so Tony and Dirk were on hand with Dom Pérignon.

Activities were pencilled into the itinerary and every hour scheduled: cocktails at a producer's apartment, theatre tickets for Streisand in *Funny Girl* and, of course, *Hello Dolly*. Dirk had already seen it but had to go again and join the captives of Carol Channing, stomping to her slow lilting descant: "Well, hello Dolly . . ." followed by a discotheque, Scotch on the rocks and doing the Jerk.

Christmas Eve, shopping on Fifth Avenue; Christmas Day a blank – and then the party was over. Eyes popping, out of dollars and missing home, I collapsed on to a late night jet at Kennedy, hand luggaging things from Saks and Bonwits for my parents, and LPs for me. Dawn came up on the Heathrow sewage farms and I was down to earth – at least physically.

My brother Edward and I were to share a mews flat over the garage where Leslie Grade's Rolls was kept in Cross Keys Close, Marylebone – two bedrooms, kitchen and bathroom, with parking meters up to the door.

I bought a large bed and a Casa Pupo bedspread, and painted my bedroom walls coffee and cream. We painted one of Eddie's walls olive green. Our windows looked on to the side of a large white glazed brick wall – it was a bit cheerless. I couldn't get cooking together, so apart from fried breakfasts we ate out.

Eddie and I were both out of work, but when anything turned up he'd go off to rep somewhere while I waited for *King Rat* to come out and for film parts. Eddie had done a production of *Hamlet*, directed by Terry Palmer, in the basement of a West End store. Terry now had the use of an old music hall theatre in Hoxton in the East End and proposed to do *Twelfth Night*.

He asked his out-of-work friends if they'd like to be in it, and we said yes, of course. Shakespeare with Terry was really enjoyable. We rehearsed in a flat in Earl's Court; Terry directed and played Feste. We had a lot of fun, getting into the text and discovering Shakespeare's theatrical skill.

I played Sir Andrew Aguecheek, because Terry decided I was really a character actor. We got people in the profession and the local Hoxton residents along, and the production was greatly appreciated. It was a most productive way of spending time out of work. However, the die of a cinema career had been cast and I didn't go for more theatrical experience, as offers from Hollywood appeared more exciting.

As a result of the strange workings of the movie world I was invited to test for an American part in Sam Spiegel's next film, *The Chase*. My connection with the film may have stemmed from working for the same studio, Columbia, the previous year in *King Rat*.

From what I could gather, Spiegel had a contract for Peter O'Toole to appear in his next picture, an option that O'Toole declined. Spiegel was committed to do a picture for Columbia with Marlon Brando, and the team of Brando and O'Toole obviously had high potential. The picture also had Arthur Penn to direct, and Jane Fonda and Robert Redford to play in it.

All these combinations seemed exciting to me, and I liked the challenge of getting out of the Guards officer mould and into something different. However, the part O'Toole had turned down was a *Dallas*-style oil millionaire's son, having an affair with the wife (Jane Fonda) of a convicted criminal (Robert Redford) who had escaped from prison and was known to be coming back to the town his wife lived in, and where the sheriff was Brando.

For obvious reasons they wanted to test me for this part. I flew out to the coast and was installed in the Beverly Wilshire Hotel, given a script and a Texas girl, Sally, to coach me in my accent. After a week of this, the accent was beginning to come, but my familiarity with the script had developed as well, and I could see that not only my part but the film as a whole had its problems.

To begin with, there was a leading star (Brando) whose role was not central to the plot, and then the sub-plot had to do with Southern racism. The main character and his wife spent two-thirds of the movie apart. Not only was the plot carelessly organised but the lines I had were almost unspeakable whatever accent you spoke them in.

It was little wonder that Arthur Penn, who was a major theatre and cinema director (*The Miracle Worker* and *Bonnie and Clyde*) decided to test me with Jane Fonda by improvising a situation in his office, instead of reading through scenes from the script.

I think it went something like this:

J: "You been drinkin', honey."
M: "Sure but . . . er . . . you know, when . . . er . . . Bubber [Redford] comes back – what'll you tell 'bout us?"
J: "Bubber loves you, baby."
M: "Sure, and he loves you too. I mean . . . what we're doing . . . he's gonna have to know about – you know what I mean?"
J: "Ssh. Be quiet. Kiss me. Oh, Jake, do you love me . . ."

And then a lot of rolling around on the carpet of Arthur's office on the fourth floor of the studio, and then back to the hotel and another 500 dollars weekly expenses while Spiegel stayed aloof in his penthouse in the Beverly Wilshire, or, as rumour had it, away in his New York apartment. I waited for a summons from the big man to tell me whether I'd passed the test or not.

From our first meeting I became very fond of Jane Fonda and she invited me for a Sunday lunch to her beach house at Malibu.

At the end of, I think, the third week I received a call from Mike Frankovich to say that they wanted me. It had been so hard to go through the ordeal that I accepted, after ringing my father, who negotiated a fee of about £20,000. Why they finally decided on me I don't know, but it was an interesting experience in the movie capital's ways and instructive as to how not to put a creative project together.

Before filming began we had a read through of the script with the whole cast, plus Mr Spiegel, on the studio floor at Columbia. When we were all gathered and had sat down at trestle tables joined together, I was seated next to Spiegel and Brando was opposite.

As we were about to begin, Brando said to Spiegel, "Sam, I thought O'Toole was meant to be in this movie."

Spiegel stared at the table and folded his hands, clearing his throat.

Brando said: "What are you kicking me for, Sam?" at which Spiegel went a plum colour and smiled sheepishly at me, while Brando might have given me the faintest of winks.

Spiegel expostulated: "You know very well, Marlon . . ." but Brando kept it up.

"No, you never told me. What's the matter, Sam? I understood O'Toole was playing Jake."

I had spent so long on the project now that I assumed the star had been informed his co-star was a non-starter. I'll never know whether Brando's surprise was sincere or not, but he certainly chose his moment to embarrass Spiegel, and I think he succeeded.

Brando kept up his enigmatic dealings with all concerned on the movie, and I, who longed to know him better and observe his ways, was frequently puzzled by his reclusive nature and apparent lack of commitment to his performance. But the results were always fascinating and his detachment may have been caused by his involvement in a production that had lost its way and was not going to be redeemed – even by the greatest acting.

This time I looked for accommodation at the beach in Malibu and was lucky to find a little two-bedroom detached house (for 400 dollars a month) just a hundred yards from where Jane lived.

As we got into the film I saw more of Jane Fonda and Roger Vadim. They were living together in Jane's beach house. I went over for meals and barbecues and I met Jane's brother Peter and his wife, and Dennis and Brook Hopper, and Bobby and Ellie Walker, and two other actor friends, Sol and Geoffrey Horne, as well as Roddy McDowall, who lived a few hundred yards further down the beach. Vadim's best friend, Christian Marquand, also came and went.

We became good friends in this convivial setting. The surf crashed down fifty yards from the rough unprotected patios, and the picnic benches and tables of the private dwellings spread along the edge of the Pacific. We sat and drank beer or listened to Dylan, and cooked barbecue meals.

Vadim played chess a lot with a rather reserved and placid manner, which seemed to belie his reputation as the world's sexiest man. Jane was eager to please him as a cook, and sometimes he would comment to the effect that one of her preparations fell a little short of his standards, but she let it pass. I've thought ever since that the French male must be a tough nut for the feminist to crack. But they were happy together and very gentle and welcoming to their friends.

During the film they surprised us all by inviting us to fly with them to Las Vegas for their wedding. We squeezed into a small private plane and flew from LA up to Nevada in a couple of hours, ending up in one of the big hotels. A registrar arrived at their hotel room and about half a dozen of us witnessed the short ceremony. Jane looked quite formal in a pretty Chanel suit of pinkish-brown weave.

We were then encouraged to enjoy Las Vegas until the plane left the following morning. They managed to get us some seats to see Sinatra and for the rest of the evening I watched the gamblers and played a little roulette. I occasionally saw Jane and Vadim at a table or playing and walking together, laughing and looking happy.

The Daisy, owned by Jack and Sally Hanson, was the best discotheque in Beverly Hills. I got to know them through a girl called Lyn and went there a few times. One evening Jack introduced me to a friend of his who was there with an actor. Her name was Amanda. We had a few dances, noticing the chagrin of her escort as we got closer.

Amanda had a blue Chevrolet. She lived alone with her mother, who was a widow. At my invitation she drove out to the beach. She looked very striking – dark hair cut short into her neck with a fringe over her forehead, dark pencil line around her beautiful green eyes. She wore a white polo-neck, short dark blue skirt, dark blue tights and shoes with a strap round the ankle. She smoked Marlboros incessantly with little short inhalations. She had delicate hands with a ring on the index finger. Underneath the clothes she was mostly bone – very thin legs, small bust, bony hips. She trotted lightly about the two-bedroomed house admiring it.

"Wow, it's really cool – how long have you had it? Do you like it? Do you live here all by yourself?"

She cooed and smiled, revealing large white teeth with a mischievous twinkle.

We tried to chat superficially but I hadn't asked her there for that and she hadn't come for that. She was as thin as a model and hardly seemed to expect tenderness or to enjoy it. She clung and seemed grateful. I felt unusually strong.

"Why were you scared?"

"I had this scene with this guy when I was in school." The guy she mentioned was a late, great comedian. I didn't ask any more questions.

A week later she gave me a new name.

"Bondo, don't brush your hair back. It looks much better forward." She laughed a little at my dark-blue suit and sports jacket and flannels.

"Hey, I – I must show you Cy Devores" – a menswear boutique on the Strip. I came away with cords and short-sleeved shirts. We went back to the beach.

As I got to know her, most things about her were an absolute contrast to Sarah. She liked to observe life, and to do that better she used to smoke, rolling her own joints in her neat way and passing them to me with, "It's cool. Haven't you smoked grass before?"

Feeling detached and peaceful, we got in the car and drove slowly and silently to Malibu Canyon. We parked, got out and began climbing large pink rocks as the sun sank like a ship, as the poet has said. They still seemed like large pink rocks to me but Amanda was entranced.

"Oh, no! How wild! Look at that! Isn't that incredible?" We made our way carefully back to the car, stopped at the supermarket on the way, filled a shopping basket and went home. I cooked an enormous steak with whole peppers on the barbecue.

"Ugh, meat," she said and made herself a salad.

The schedule on the film was fairly light for me. I had scenes with E. G. Marshall, who played my dad, and who had inspired me with his performance in *Twelve Angry Men*, and with Brando, who listened, waited and then spoke more into the beyond than to me.

I acted with Jane in a motel bedroom scene where I was clutching a champagne bottle, and we repeated our wrestling match from Arthur Penn's office, only this time being a bit more careful not to upset her hairdo.

Finally we got to the big climax of the picture, where Redford, Jane and I all met up at a used car dump which the locals set fire to, which resulted in my being crushed by a falling axle.

Considering that the film also had Janice Rule, Angie Dickinson and Robert Duvall, it should have been very powerful. Redford was already acknowledged as a new find and they were obviously hoping that *The Chase* would make him a star, but he was only able to give a glimpse of his possibilities in it. To me his quality is found in his attitude to his private life. He was independent and resourceful enough to build his own home in the mountains of Utah and to spend his time there rather than in Hollywood or New York when he was not working.

Amanda and I hired a car and went to San Francisco for a week after the film was over. We were looking for the beat scene of Haight Ashbury but only saw the streets and tourist sights like Chinatown, the Bridge and the Bay, as well as one of the homosexual discotheques which flourished there.

By now we were making plans for Amanda to come and stay with me over Christmas in London, at my parents' home. I left LA feeling involved and settled in an important new relationship. Love letters and telephone calls flowed. I sent her the price of the ticket, and then at last came the longed-for day when she skipped up to the exit barrier at London Airport and into my life again.

Amanda was as fascinated by the King's Road as I had been by Malibu. I took her to my parents and she met relations. Everything from aunts to eccentric tramps was a complete delight. We went to Cornwall and stayed in the seaside cottage my parents had built at Fowey. As we were smoking and seeing everything through that rather detached view that pot induces, my mother's verdict was that we were both in cloud-cuckoo-land.

Since I didn't know what I wanted for our relationship, she slipped back to LA early in the New Year and I went back to living with my brother Ed in Cross Keys Close. Late one night the phone rang and an operator from Los Angeles asked me if I was James Fox and could I take a call.

This time it wasn't Amanda but Ross Hunter, who had a part he wanted me for in a musical, *Thoroughly Modern Millie*, to be made at Universal Studios, playing a comedy role opposite Julie Andrews.

I was glad of the proposal as it also gave me a chance to

get back to Amanda, and I was delighted with the prospect of a totally different part. I gave Ross a quick "Yes".

We had two weeks' rehearsals, principally for the dancing. Ross had engaged Joe Leyton, one of America's most gifted choreographers. The number that he created for me was called the Tapioca. I suspect that the feet and hand movements interpreting the Tap-tap-tap-tapioca and the Slap-slap-slap-slapioca of the lyrics owed a good deal to his observation of my gangling gait. It was wonderful fun. Disappointingly, they dubbed a more perfect singing voice instead of using mine on the soundtrack.

The character of Jimmy came really easily under the influence of George Roy Hill's deft sense of style and period. We saw a few Harold Lloyd films and decided on a kind of fresh-faced, whizz-bang, carefree kid approach.

Bea Lillie was a little frail, but we all stood around crying with laughter at her Mrs Meers, the owner of a little hotel where girls were drugged and sold to the white slave trade. In one scene she drugged Mary Tyler Moore's fruit drink and offered it to her. She was about to drink it and Bea was saying 'cheers' when Mary was called away to dance. At the same time other dancers put their drinks down on the tray and Bea was left gazing at the glasses with one eyebrow raised. Quite unexpectedly she suddenly started to move them like draughtsmen, jumping three glasses in a row to finish it off. It was brilliantly inspired business.

My critical faculties switch off when it comes to Carol Channing. She played this wonderful, enthusiastic Broadway lady. Everything was so huge, so much fun and so over the top that she was untoppable. For a while afterwards in her TV interviews she used to send greetings to that 'dear Jimmy Fox'. How can you resist that?

I wish I'd paid more attention to the way she holds her audience. A lot of it is sheer professionalism of course. I have a strange collection of memories of her – the amazing mink eyelashes, her kangaroo meat diet and her husband, who was constantly at her elbow because she is rather short-sighted. He would be whispering in her ear, "Here comes the head of the studio," and Carol would beam, "H-E-L-L-O, Lou."

"On your right, your co-star Mary Tyler Moore."

"M-A-R-Y."

The film itself was completed in precisely sixteen weeks and we felt it all went very smoothly. Julie carried it with her 'flapper' performance – one she had perfected before in *The Boy Friend* on Broadway.

She is a dominating performer but a generous one. There was one scene in a restaurant where we ended up washing the dishes because, under the pretence of being a poor kid, I couldn't find the money to pay the bill. I thought it would be in character if, at this point, I did a bit of juggling with the plates. I practised this for six weeks with three tin plates and announced to George on the day of the scene that I had this little bit of business I would like to do.

Julie looked sideways at me. After all, we had lines to say and it was a scene where there wasn't a lot of hanging about. Nevertheless she said, "OK". We did a couple of takes: the plates flew all right and I even caught the last one behind my back. Being with Julie Andrews encourages you to achieve things you didn't know you could do!

When I knew I was going out to Hollywood again I asked Amanda to find a house at the beach for us. She couldn't get a place in Malibu but found one further towards Santa Monica on Pacific Coast Highway. She wanted to take up photography, so we bought a 35 mm Nikon. In fact, we went to Tijuana on the Mexico-United States border in order to take pictures of the Spanish bullfighter El Cordobes.

We began living together. Amanda had a waifish charm and originality, but what captured me totally was the way she never seemed to want to hold on to me too closely. We both wanted to educate ourselves and experience all the opportunities that were open to us together.

Two other people who enjoyed Amanda's beauty and personality were Christopher Isherwood and Don Bachardy. We used to visit them in Santa Monica and Don did a splendid picture of her which conveyed her strange allure marvellously.

When the Rolling Stones came over to Los Angeles that summer, Amanda and a friend found out where they were staying and went to the hotel to try and meet them. She turned me on to the Stones' music.

By the end of *Thoroughly Modern Millie*, my career had reached a high point. I was a 50,000-dollar-a-film star, in demand in the United States and England, and a name on the marquee.

After *Millie*, Amanda and I went to Mexico for three weeks and then left for London where we stayed with a friend, Peter Eyre, in his flat off the King's Road. We 'scored some gear', to use the current phrase: large floppy hats, long narrow patterned scarves, silky shirts. At that time London was the pop music, clothes and LSD capital of the world.

But at this point, in August 1966, I decided to take a break from films and go with Amanda to live in Rome.

7

ROME

Why did I go to Rome? I think there are three reasons – for obscurity, for culture and for *la dolce vita*.

One of the results of becoming famous or successful is that very often it makes people want to be just an ordinary indistinguishable person again. Not that I had reached the stage where I could not enter a restaurant without provoking a disturbance, but I still felt somewhat public. Rome provided a chance to merge, to disappear, to become real.

The cultural reason for going to Rome was more practical. I had felt starved in the plastic culture of Los Angeles. Rome to us was the place to discover artistic first principles. We were excited at the prospect of visiting the galleries and churches, seeing the buildings and being caught up in its ancient beauty. I think I wanted to discover the meaning of life as the Renaissance had interpreted it – and to me the Renaissance had got it right.

Lastly but more unconsciously we sought *la dolce vita*, Rome's *fa niente* (do nothing) attitude, its beautiful people and shops, its tolerance of those who wanted to live carefreely.

I really found I didn't miss the offer of parts, the wooing and the wheeling and dealing for my services, nor the recognition of my performance, but I could not do without the money that my fame had brought. A regular injection of bank transfers to keep us alive was needed, and although we didn't live luxuriously, we always seemed to be at the post office for a new draft.

Our flat was a two-bedroomed one at the top of a little, modern four-storey building opposite the Church of San

Andrea delle Fratte. A friend, George Hayim, had got it for us through a friend of his, Felicity Mason. For what it was, it was quite expensive. I had to pay our cleaning lady, I ran a rather thirsty dark-blue Jaguar 3.8S, and we usually ate out every meal.

I recall a rather dotty thing I used to do with regard to my Jag. It had the most beautiful wire wheels with large nuts you had to knock off and on with a brass-headed hammer. I would carry my wheels one at a time up to our little balcony, and spend a long time rubbing between the spokes to shine them up. I suppose it was sheer vanity – just to see the wheels glinting at night, parked under a Roman street light or in a beautiful piazza. It was a sight!

The car had a 45 r.p.m. record player installed and we kept the sounds going on Arthur Connolly, Sam and Dave, Otis Redding, Mick and the Stones and Marianne Faithfull.

Our Roman life was not especially social but we met Paul and Talitha Getty and some Italian friends called Tomeucci, with whom we went on holiday to Cortina, and another sweet girl, Laura, who showed us around. We took Italian lessons and progressed a little. At least I became adept at reading a menu and doing the shopping. We had all the time we wanted to explore the fountains of civilisation.

Probably my favourite place was Florence. You could start at the top with Brunelleschi's wondrous cathedral dome, and, standing beside it, see the pink and green stoned elegance of Giotto's bell tower. It was enough to take your breath away.

Turning our backs on the cathedral, as the guidebooks would say, and walking a few paces, we would crane round the dozens of tourists admiring Ghiberti's Baptistry door, its deep bronze reliefs depicting scenes from the Old Testament. But the feast was only beginning. As I passed by the Botticellis in the Uffizi I could have been looking at faces by David Bailey in his Book of Pin-Ups. Perhaps London was in the process of Renaissance.

I decided that Botticelli had escaped from the system of religious topics and his art with its mythical themes was much more lively, earthly and sensual. Not that one could say he was any better than the wonderful Fra Angelico or Filippo Lippi, but there was in Botticelli – and Raphael – an evidently secular spirit. Whatever it meant to be a Renaissance man, I felt I was one.

The same was true of Donatello's John the Baptist, and Michelangelo's David. To see the latter's David and his unfinished figures emerging from the marble, or, back in Rome, to look upwards to the ceiling of the Sistine Chapel, made me recognise not only what talent but also what effort had been required. Michelangelo seemed free to portray Creation on the ceiling and the Last Judgment on the end wall with an unrestrained imagination.

Art, then, is a feature of Italian life. So, more prosaically, are trousers. I had two excellent pairs made by the top trouser lady, Signora Romognoli, tight across the hips and hanging straight from the thighs. To go with these I bought some flowered Liberty cotton material and had it made up into matching shirts and ties. On the Via Frattina I found a lovely velvet jacket and brown Italian casuals, with a belt.

Pot and hash weren't easily available in Rome, so, as we were also anxious to see Morocco for ourselves, we accepted Paul and Talitha's invitation to stay at their Villa in Marrakesh. They had a beautiful walled home with a central courtyard richly floored with Moroccan tiles and a fountain. Off it were the principal living rooms, their walls, floors and ceilings covered with symmetrical patterns, inlaid with tiles or covered with Arabic velvet hangings.

We were served mint tea by a quietly efficient befezzed head servant in an immaculate white linen ankle-length kaftan. The Moroccan lifestyle was rich and relaxing and, for hippy Westerners like ourselves, offered the perfect environment in which to get stoned.

The elaborate pipe filled with *kif* was passed around the circle. Its effect was to render all of us inactive. Very few decisions were made, except perhaps to go and eat. We just gazed at the complicated patterns or watched the amused delight or intense concentration of our companions as another pipe was prepared.

But I did not find the effects so relaxing. Being under the influence of the drug made me uneasy. I did not want to let go of my rational control. I felt there was an evil, accusing presence making me unable to enjoy the company or the activity. I also became suspicious and fearful, a condition which was described as paranoid by my truly affectionate companions. They encouraged me to let go and enjoy the experience.

With two friends, Mark Palmer and Denis Deagen, we decided to hire a car and take a look at Rabat and Fez. Having paid for the hire I took the wheel. After an hour or so, just when it was getting drowsily hot in the early afternoon, I dozed off as I was going down a long stretch of road. I woke up just in time to avoid slamming with full force into a parked farm vehicle. We didn't avoid contact altogether, however, and it left me very shaken.

We continued on our tour, taking in the sights of Morocco's most beautiful and oldest city, Fez. We not only used the local brew to smoke, but tripped with some powerful American chemical called STP; it offered a short trip which seemed to turn your mind into one of those kaleidoscopes children used to look into, where the patterns changed as you shook the little coloured grains against the angled prisms at the end.

Not only was I in a guilty muddle about drugs, but my sexual imagination was also in a turmoil. We went back to Rome with our kaftans and our rugs, having tasted *la vie marocaine*.

Amanda and I decided to get engaged at Christmas, and we rang my parents to tell them. They were clearly worried about what I was doing, but couldn't do much about it. My father, who was representing me as my agent, suggested I accept an invitation to the New York opening of *Thoroughly Modern Millie* and that I should get back to work in 1968.

In New York we consolidated our freaky lifestyle but for

the first time I realised how dangerous it was to possess drugs. Stories constantly circulated of police busts and of pop stars like the Stones being raided.

We saw the Doors play live, visited Andy Warhol in his pop-art lair, sat around in the Drake Hotel with Terry Southern and met William Burroughs.

My mildly hippy appearance attracted the editor of *Vogue* who commissioned one of New York's top photographers, Irving Penn, to photograph the back of my head for the magazine. She particularly liked the way my hair grew; it was 1968 and long hair was still intriguing in the USA.

Back in Rome there was time to think again. By now I had begun to question who I really was, what governed the things that I did and what I wanted to achieve in life.

I wrote in my diary in Rome, Saturday, April 29th:

I am in the grip of a fearful realisation which frightens me even now of the wasteful, evil life into which I have let myself fall. I, who would five years ago have looked at my present situation with compassion and anxiety, am now in a pre-planned hell which has come upon me like a creeping black plague which contaminates the victim without apparently affecting him but which gives his friends and others horrible intimations of the most probable end towards which he must go. I was driven here mostly out of loneliness and out of admiration for what looked exciting but which is dangerous. The way to happiness is not found on the youthful trips of crazy imaginations.

My girlfriend is a messenger who has been sent to encourage me to do things that won't bring good to all whom I love. And yet she is not the cause, she is the companion, the procurer, the aid, the initiator. I am the willing subject, now tormented, but before, searching for a rich, uncommitted, contemptuous, spoilt fling, thinking it could lead towards self-improvement. Let's say that is all our aims, the one of self-perfection, or feeding one's pleasure senses until we think we have felt ecstacy, the kind we can't feel in an ordinary life doing ordinary things.

Well, beware, my friend. If you don't stop wanting this kind of escape you will find the truth too hard to bear.

But what I've started is already too late to stop, carrying around masses of drugs for me and other people. For what purpose? To forget, to conceal, to be big, to be cool, to join in, to drop out, anything rather than to be myself and, in trying, to fail in that. I am doing myself a big disfavour because if I could really say that this is a beautiful way to live I would unhesitatingly continue to live this way.

If the police wanted to extract an anti-drugs statement from me I would tell them that it was not the job of the police to discriminate on the question of taste of the generation that is turning on. If they consider drugs dangerous and harmful then I would say yes to those who can't take them like me. And therefore potentially everybody is in danger while they are around by being threatened with contact with someone who wants to turn them on.

But, let me not blame drugs for what is wrong in my case. That goes back quite a lot further. I seem to remember to the time when I first began to avoid involvement with *work*, or study, or practice. The core of the disease is the desire to escape. The danger of drugs is that it helps in this. Where drugs are found, there too is idleness, laziness, inconsistency, deceit, ugliness. They promote gatherings in groups so that all may feel not too afraid because of the company of others whom they look up to.

Well, looking up to others of this kind is very easy and very stupid because they don't have anyone's interest at heart but their own. If one wants to look up to someone, why not look up to Jesus Christ, Mohammed, Florence Nightingale, St Francis, Socrates and Buddha. Take the real heroes and saints and copy them.

A month later, on June 1st, I wrote the following:

The present or the moment at which I write this is rather a difficult time in which to tell you exactly how it feels to be alive. The present has always been the most real and impressionable moment for me and it has the effect of making very enjoyable experiences and rather awful ones intensified.

My definition of enjoyable and awful are rather peculiar. Sharing something with one I love, learning something new, giving unselfishly but discriminatingly (I rather hate to say that), being satisfied: these are four things that give me pleasure. The things that give me pain: loneliness; insecurity; not laying foundations; reflecting on things like – when are you sad – knowing what I should do and not doing it; wasting my time with silly people; regretting; not being able to give a good answer for my behaviour that will satisfy me longer than the time it takes to do it.

I'm twenty-eight. What my schoolmaster said to me, that my attitude was all wrong, has basically not changed. I've always felt crucially that what I felt was best – and have put up with, but only just that – what was also clearly thought and adhered to by many others. It comes partly from what I do, but not only, because what I did when I was quite poor as a teenager and in the early twenties was just to try and do the same things as I do now, but without the funds.

And now I feel a big change coming over me. I'm not afraid to give up the small success I've had in films for a serious career in the theatre (sounds a bit cold). I mean, I want to give myself, my talent and my mind to be trained, to perform before audiences. I find that yoga and meditation are not good for me at this minute. I'm hell-bent on finding things to dislike about myself and to examining minutely my physical and mental set-up just leads to more depression. No, the real saviour is loss of self, subordination of ego to – something bigger. That something bigger is now what I'm looking for. I've one enemy to conquer, idleness; another, complacency; another, fear of new and sudden change (of giving up what I have stored), but I know this now at least and therefore can fight it.

I decided I should get around to reading the New Testament again but meanwhile life in Rome was getting more diverting. The Rolling Stones, who were making a European tour, came to Rome and through going to their concert with the Gettys we met Mick Jagger, Brian Jones and the rest. Mick invited us to the concert and we were in his back-stage entourage. Rome was at his feet, and the Stones shook the conventional Italian teenagers with their anarchic strut. We took them out to Jane and Vadim's about 1 a.m. and lay around smoking. Amanda disappeared – and Mick was also out of the room. I was caught by emotions of jealousy and curiosity. She came back starry-eyed and stoned.

We drove to the Colosseum in a Fellini-like dream. We clambered over the ancient pitted stones, shouted in the vaulty wastes and tripped in our imaginations on the chariot races and blood-thirsty crowds. We had been taking uppers as well and we crashed back at Jane and Vadim's hungry for more love-making.

Being around the Stones for those few days was like being on a trip. Night and day lost their identity. Events had their aura. People were bewitchingly interesting. I was attracted towards them and, having been drawn in, something was imparted to me also. I felt elite and powerful, high on energy. Having been a fan of the Stones for a year, my expectation had already been created. 'Going Home', 'Ruby Tuesday' and 'Baby, You're Out of Time' were played all day long.

Their arrival, I suppose, signalled for me a return to my work. The sheer creative excitement generated an enthusiasm and a desire to leave obscurity and return to where it was all happening – London. But I wasn't to return to work immediately. The captivating power of my new life was too great for that.

We rented a flat near Marble Arch; one day Mick came over and brought by a record which he liked – 'A Whiter Shade of Pale' by Procul Harem. We identified completely with this surreal song and its fugal sound. Our circle of friends were the beautiful trippers. We collected Arthur Rackham's illustrations, hung our rooms with Moroccan drapes and adorned ourselves with hats, scarves and butterfly brooches.

On another occasion we went with Mick and Marianne Faithfull to a reception Dirk was having at the Connaught for the film *Accident*. We were the odd ones out in this rather respectable film people's circle. I felt distanced from the show-biz world. They seemed to be involved in rather false social behaviour and stagnant film ideas. I wanted to be able to tell them this and felt much closer to the outspoken honesty of the Stones and the 'pop' scene. We sat on the radiators giggling and snapping amyl-nitrite capsules. Dirk came across and told me that if I wanted to do that kind of thing to do it in the loo.

In the heat of June there burst on to the scene the Beatles' psychedelic masterpiece 'Sergeant Pepper's Lonely Hearts' Club Band'. I remember sending Paul a telegram: 'It should be played on loudspeakers all day in Hyde Park.'

I found when I visited people's homes that due to the general trend to be tripping a lot of the time they didn't take much notice of you. If you were not 'spaced out' yourself you simply had to adapt to the atmosphere, join the quiet, introverted company and not destroy the peaceful vibes with conversation.

My spirit was not often at peace. I remember one night at Christopher Gibbs' house on the Embankment, amid the ornate and sombre surroundings and the beautiful and intelligent flower of the hip aristocracy, a deep sense of foreboding and gloom came on me as we passed the pot, a mood which Christopher detected and kindly sought to assuage.

I had already met Donald Cammell that summer, and he now came to discuss his screenplay, *Duffy*, with me. He wanted me to play a hippy amateur heister who hires an American pro to help him rob some gold from a ship belonging to his father. Bob Parrish directed it and James Coburn played the American master thief with a penchant for modern art. I agreed to do it mostly out of friendship and admiration for Donald. I was back in acting again. In fact, the dramatic events of the past six months of my life had provided the background for this present role.

Amanda didn't come with me when I went to start filming in Spain. Through the summer we had begun to break up. We had had a *liaison dangereuse*. I was both repelled and attracted by our pursuits. Her influence on me had been profound. I had changed. I had drawn away from a straight acting career. I had become mildly hippy. My behaviour had even provoked my father to launch a really violent attack on my lifestyle. Through Amanda I had become ironical, detached and experimental. I believe she loved me, which was what I wanted, but I was also trying to understand myself and instead I was only getting more confused. But the break-up was indecisive and dragged on. She stayed in London where I tried to phone her many times to sort it out. But in fact I did not know what I wanted.

Filming was thus made harder. One thing was clear – Donald had a tremendous talent, but he needed control of the production if his ideas were to be properly interpreted. On *Duffy* he was only the script-writer, but his chance came a year later, when he not only wrote but also co-directed *Performance*.

Intending to try to forget the break-up I was glad when my father came to me soon afterwards with the part of Gordon Craig in Karel Reisz's *Isadora*. Gordon Craig was a 1904 hippy – he and Isadora Duncan had an affair and inspired one another's art, then separated after having two children. I was thrilled to work with Vanessa Redgrave, though I didn't feel on my best form in a part which in my view could have been more developed.

In fact, I felt frustrated in the part. I had researched the background quite thoroughly and in my view the script did not develop the destructiveness nor the artistic implications of the lovers' relationship. The film covered Isadora's three great love affairs and the Gordon Craig character was sacrificed.

I had been on the film about six weeks when there was a month's break for me from it, from late February to early April. This free period enabled me to accept an invitation from the Brazilian film board to go with Trevor Howard and others as guests to the Rio de Janeiro carnival for ten days. I didn't know then, as I left Gatwick Airport, that I would never complete *Isadora*.

8

THE AMAZON

Duffy was not an especially happy experience. I upset the director and producer by being too much in character and somewhat critical of Hollywood's interpretation of the hippy scene in Europe. However, through what I earned from it and *Isadora* I was able to buy a house.

Some friends of mine heard of this beautiful private park in Wandsworth which was surrounded by Victorian houses, each of which had access to it. I heard of one going on the market belonging to a Mrs Blackwell; I looked her up.

The house, 3 Spencer Park, was built entirely of concrete and had a flat roof. It had an eighty-foot-long garden and needed a lot doing to it. I had made friends with Rikki Huston, John Huston's ex-wife, who had in my view very original ideas on decoration and who promised to help me. I lived in one of the six bedrooms while we engaged a structural engineer to remove an interior concrete wall. As things weren't too comfortable while the building was being done, I hoped to spend much of the time away.

Before I left England, Donald Cammell also told me he was writing a picture for Mick Jagger and myself called *The Performers*, which he would finish by May, and it would involve my playing the part of a South London villain.

England's snowy fields slipped away below me and we journeyed on over miles of ever-brightening seas towards the Equator. The blast of Brazil's heat hit us as we descended the plane's steps in Rio. We were met by a friendly young interpreter called Christina Alvarino and were taken to a big old-fashioned hotel on the Copacabana beach. We got our timetable, went out for a meal, unpacked and collapsed.

Christina's family were keen on yachting and so she took us next day for a drink to the yacht club. It was an attractive place on the harbour with a view of the famous Sugar Loaf Mountain, friendlier than the hotel and a good place to come to cool off and get a drink in the midst of our publicity interviews and generally hectic programme.

Christina invited me to her home and also showed me many of the sights. One of them was a *favella*, a sort of refugee camp made up of rickety dwellings, built of wood and corrugated iron, where hundreds of very poor families and children lived. It was these very poor who were the main participants in the carnival.

The crowning event was the big street parade at night. The Brazilians dressed themselves in their home-made costumes, the most elaborate of which took them a whole year to make and cost them a considerable amount of money. Some of them, in the style of the eighteenth century Spanish and European aristocracy, wore enormous powdered white wigs piled above their shining brown faces and great billowing ball-gowns. They rode in gilt carriages, while others chose the brightly coloured costumes of the peasant people and walked.

Everywhere people were jumping and dancing to the incessant drum beat. No one could keep still; the town carried on day and night without a rest for as long as everyone could remain upright.

I met Peter Clifford in the yacht club on about the third day of the carnival. He had been up for about three nights and declared he was just about getting into it. He had arrived in Rio having been crew on a yacht in an ocean race from Buenos Aires. Peter was English, about twenty-four, and was taking some time off from law studies to travel. Ocean racing and bob-sleighing were his other interests, and he had represented Great Britain at both. We struck up a friendship.

Peter had already worked out his next assignment – to

see the Altiplano region of the Andes, around La Paz in Bolivia, and especially Machu Picchu, the 15,000 foot Inca retreat in Peru, and then to follow one of the small tributaries of the Amazon, the Beni, from far up in the Andes where it rises, down into the forest, into the River Mamore, and on the Amazon up to Manaus, 1,500 miles away.

He had heard that Colonel Fawcett, an Englishman, had made the same trip when he had been making maps of the area and had used a balsa-wood raft on the narrow fast-flowing rivers. Peter wanted to use the same method. He also informed me that Colonel Fawcett had disappeared in that region.

He asked me if I'd like to come, too. My first reaction was to jump at it, but then I realised that I had a film contract to finish on *Isadora*. Nevertheless I said: "Yes. Why not?" I'm afraid I did not regard the Roman temple sequence in *Isadora* as sufficient reason to turn down this expedition. I acted wrongly in taking Peter up on it, but I didn't see it that way at the time.

Peter was really delighted to have a companion and decided we should set about getting a team together. Meanwhile I cabled my dad in London that I intended to stay in Rio and go on a trip up the Amazon. On both counts he must have been considerably concerned at this news. He cabled back that he was coming out to Rio.

Obviously his first reaction must have been that I was on a very heavy drug trip and needed to be rescued. I could see from his expression as he got off the plane that he was ready to take on the local mafia, if necessary, or anybody else who was blowing his son's mind. After meeting the Alvarino family, Peter and some others, he began to look a bit less worried.

He was tired and still wearing his office clothes.

"Why can't you finish the picture and then come and do your trip?" he asked.

"If I don't do it now, I will never do it," I replied.

Still, he tried his hardest to persuade me to abandon this

risky venture and come back to England to fulfil my professional commitments.

As I was twenty-nine at the time we were talking as friends as much as father and son. His reasons could not prevail against my determination. Dejectedly he flew home and I was left to work out the consequences of my decision.

Peter had, by this time, been recruiting another man – Ian Reid, an Australian cattle farmer taking two years away from home to travel and study the Santa Cruzeiros breed of Argentinian cattle. He was in his early twenties, built like a short-horn steer, and responded to the idea with enthusiasm. The last few days in Rio were spent planning a route to La Paz in Bolivia, checking train times and saying goodbye to the Alvarinos, who had shown us great hospitality.

We entrained for the first leg of the trip down to São Paulo, a sprawling city of seven million people in 1968. My first priority was to buy a pair of real South American cowboy boots. I found a pair after our first night in a fairly basic midtown hotel. Peter said that hotels were too expensive and things would have to change. His footwear for the jungle was a pair of 'tennies' that did him anywhere and everywhere. The same day we boarded a train for the Bolivian border, a journey which took a day and a night, across flat, sparsely populated farming country.

The contrast between the two countries at the border was noticeable. The Brazilian town of Corumbá was mostly two-storey buildings with streets and pavements, served by transport, lit by street lamps, busy with the bustle of shoppers and small town activity. But when we drove over the border to the nearest village of Puerto Suárez the scene was different: single storey huts, no streets, pavements, electricity, shops or signs, only a small bar, the odd truck or motor scooter, and the town's water supply being fetched at dusk from the nearby flooded ground in round drums on a cart pulled by oxen.

Peter's promise that the hotel accommodation would change was fulfilled with interest. Hotels were non-existent in this place. There wasn't even an inn. We searched up the

Leading Ladies
With Sarah Miles in *The Servant* (above) and Susannah York in *Duffy*
(below).

Those Magnificent Men . . .
An impressive figure in full dress uniform in a scene from *Those Magnificent
Men in their Flying Machines*.

'My Best Role to Date' . . .

. . . James Fox in scenes from *Performance* with Mick Jagger. It was to be his last film role for ten years (above, below and previous page).

Settling Down

Above: Congratulations from elder brother Edward on James' marriage to Mary Piper.

Below left: The Navigators: on the beach with a group of Sheffield students during his years as a Christian teacher.

Below right: No longer Alone: A film from the Billy Graham Organisation released in 1977.

Family Man
With Mary and his four children.

Today's Focus

Above: James with his brothers Edward and Robert. *Below left:* Angela Fox. *Below right:* In a scene from *Country:* the BBC play that reintroduced him to the viewing public.

Comeback Roles

Right: With Lisa Harrow from *Nancy Astor*.

Left: James in Russian guise with Galina Baleva in a scene from *A Woman for all Time*, based on the life of Anna Pavlova, and due for release shortly.

Right: With Jane Asher in *Love is Old, Love is New*.

one main street followed by stray dogs and curious children and found a front room that had a bed or two in it. We tossed for the floor and sank down.

My heart had sunk too at our situation. The flies bit, there was no proper place to eat and nothing on the beds. It was all made even harder by the fresh remembrance of where we had just come from! But surprisingly we managed to sleep and with the light all seemed better. We felt that if we could make this adjustment, it could only be training for what lay ahead. After another day there, we got to the bus and started from the next town on the long haul from sea level up 15,000 feet to the highest capital city in the world.

Contrasts were in order again: a river in the foothills of the Andes was in flood and had swept over the road. We got out to see if there was a way across and the bus driver picked his way through the mud and swirling waters. Our destination on this first bus was Cochabamba at 8,000 feet. Coming to our first Bolivian town we were greeted by sights new to our eyes — women wearing large bowler hats and people of Indian appearance. Another fresh sensation was the temperature, which had dropped considerably.

We had seen the beautiful llama grazing gently beside the roads as we got higher up into the mountains and now we were able to buy a couple of beautiful hand-made llama ponchos. Even Peter invested in one of these.

The Altiplano, as it is called, the high flat plain on the top of the Andes, is quite bewitching. Its magic is distilled in the eerie pipe music of the local people, which soars like the majestic uplands whence it comes. Its people, with their grey-brown, taut-skinned faces, chewing away at their intoxicating leaves and enduring these strange heights in their brightly coloured llama-wool garments, are unforgettable.

Finally, drawing our breath hard because of the thinness of the air, we reached La Paz. Our first port of call was the Overseas Students' Club, where we found a German boy who kindly agreed to put us up in his flat, and an American named Gaucho Smatla. Gaucho was on a two-year assignment with the Peace Corps. We explained our mission to him and over a meal asked if he'd like to come with us, first to Machu Picchu and then to the Beni. He had some weeks' leave due and liked the sound of the trip. He could speak some Spanish and was used to roughing it. His appearance was lanky, with some fair bumfluff for a moustache, and he wore a black stetson. No one had much trouble guessing where he came from.

Depositing all but our kitbags, we set out by bus to Lake Titicaca which we had to cross to get to Peru. At 12,500 feet this huge inland lake is the highest navigable piece of water in the world and is served by a lovely old ferry boat built, I think, in Hull in 1907 and still running smoothly. It was a day and a night trip across the lake, sailing beneath the stars.

First call in Peru was Cuzco, an ancient Inca settlement colonised by the Spanish, from where the Incas had fled into the jungle to escape the *conquistadores*, greedy for their gold. Setting out in the morning we then followed their journey by bus through the dense lofty trees, deeper and deeper into uninhabitable forest. Later the same day we reached the mountain village of Machu Picchu, the last Inca outpost, where a remnant of the race remained undisturbed by the Spaniards.

Situated on a hillside cleared for cultivation, not very large in size, it still bore evidence of a past civilisation and the cult of a now extinct people, who worshipped the sun and were ruled by a priestly class who cultivated the steep hills by terraced farming.

It was deeply impressive to see how the priests exercised influence over the people by predicting how far the sun would cast its shadow on the longest day of the year, measured on a stone that is still there. And it was also impressive to think about their relationship to the sun, on their island of land cut out of the jungle 12,500 feet up near the Equator.

With our imaginations and our cameras filled, we turned in at the one cheap sleeping-place provided, and never slept better or closer to the stars. If the Beni could top that, we were going to have a great time. We made our way thoughtfully back to La Paz, wondering about this lost Indian civilisation and whether any of its people had survived in the noble-looking present-day Peruvians.

In La Paz it was time to equip ourselves for the trip. I hadn't exactly come prepared for the Altiplano or the jungle in my Michael Fish shirts and white trousers, but clothing was not the only item which needed renewing. To start with, I was advised by our consulate that I needed typhus, TAB and malaria shots, and I also bought some penicillin capsules and throw-away syringes, as well as some anti-snakebite serum and alcohol.

Thinking about the possible dangers we discussed what weapons we needed to take. I had about 750 dollars in cash, given to me for use during the festival, which we reckoned should be plenty for the trip, so I contributed the lion's share towards the shotgun and some ammunition. Ian bought himself a .38 revolver. Gaucho chose a machete (more for hacking his way than for self-defence, we hoped).

I wanted to make a film record of the trip, so I bought a secondhand 8mm Kodak and some film from a German supplier, a Dr Schilling, who had made a trip to the same region. He invited us to his home to see some movies and meet yet another German – a hunter – who was very knowledgeable about the Beni.

This man gave us information about two different journeys he could recommend and advised us on equipment. When he discovered that none of us spoke much Spanish, he said he would give us one essential piece of advice: "When you talk to the Indian people – smile!"

I was particularly worried about the food situation, so we took a large sack to the shops and bought eight large tins of tuna, eight of corned beef, a large container for water, eight cans of soup, bags of rice, tins of Nestlé's condensed milk, a jar of honey, chewing gum and a bottle of gin. We reckoned that would be enough for twenty-one days.

The shopping list was still not complete. Only Gaucho

had equipment for camping, so we bought mosquito nets, sleeping bags, ground sheets, blankets, hammocks, a cooking stove, eating tins and utensils, Ajax powder, soap, a lamp, compass, torch and large rubber bags to keep our equipment dry on the raft, together with a line and a waterbottle.

For the mind I bought a copy of Winston Churchill's wartime speeches, *The Razor's Edge* by Somerset Maugham, *The Magic Mountain* by Thomas Mann, a James Bond and a phrase book.

We needed re-entry visas for Brazil, and for my cash I bought a little money belt. I sent a letter to my solicitor, bearing in mind the dangers of the trip, and postcards to Mrs Riley, who was my daily help at Spencer Park, and a few friends and family, telling them of my plans.

There were final discussions with our German friend on the route from Rurrenabaque where our balsa wood raft trip was to end, and advice from Professor Bruntweer, who owned a pharmacy, on what film to buy: "*Das Kodak macht das grün zu tief*" he warned. Then, at last, humping a great sack of wood with us, we gathered early in the morning at the bus station.

By 11.30 we were over the dripping, slipping Andes and by 3 p.m. on the first day down 6,000 feet to Coronari and then to a gold-mining camp at Teoponte on the Beni the next day. Our trip was to start from there.

The river was about 100 yards wide and fast flowing at that point. The camp, built and run by an American company, was hospitable and well equipped. The Americans operated the dredge and the Bolivians had checking officers. We were told they lifted 150,000 dollars' worth of gold a month from the river bed, but to do this the dredge had to keep going day and night.

Our guide's raft had to be sought out upstream. We walked seven kilometres to Tipuani and through the American padre contacted the head waterman, who took us to one man who was too expensive and then another who asked 100 dollars (1,200 pesos) for the trip. We agreed and like fools gave Figueredu 600 pesos in advance. He was to get the raft ready and then come to the mining camp for us. We went back to the village for the night.

Ian had his .38 in his holster and the local police came and took it from him. The padre used his influence with the mayor and the next day we retrieved it. Presumably we looked suspicious, especially since we were not far from where Che Guevara had made his last stand just six months before.

We fooled about on the river with some rubber-coated flour bags which we had inflated, and hanging on to them let the current take us downstream. I filmed Ian, Gaucho and Peter who, in the end, became expert enough to 'bag' through rapids.

A week went by and our guide still hadn't arrived, so we trudged back to his village and called at his house. He had two wives and eight children and they assured us that he was not at home. One wife took off to look for him. She walked purposefully to the river, raised her hand to shield her eyes and scanned the shimmering waters for signs of Fig. But Peter found him at his mum's, looking as right as a rain forest and meowing like a cat: "Mañana . . ."

"Ahora!" ("Now!") we shouted back at him in unison and pushed him towards his suitcase. Once he saw there was no escape he gave in. We also met his number two guide, Julio, who looked a good man. Closely watched by us they packed quickly, assembled a small raft out of four balsa logs, and – closely followed by us on our inflated bags – pushed themselves out into the flowing current.

At 5.30 p.m., after they had spent an hour attaching a few side logs, we left Teoponte. The tiny raft was fully laden, with decks awash, six people on it, our luggage in the plastic bags on which four of us perched. Julio was the bowman with Fig at the stern, both with paddles.

Soon we were into our first rapid. The distant rumble which greeted our ears brought cries and commands, and then we were broadside on to the flood, looking rather badly positioned. Slowly the bow was pushed upstream, despite Julio's efforts, and in this way we started going through the white surf. It completely covered the balsa, the luggage and half of us. I waved my camera in the general direction of the action. It was all very exciting. When it was over we pulled ashore and slept intermittently in a shack.

The following day, for the largest rapid on the river, only Peter, the two guides and the luggage remained on board. Standing on the bank I photographed them dipping and rising between the giant boulders.

At night we slept under the mosquito nets in the open on the sloping beach by the river. For tea we collected muddy river water and boiled it, and added tea leaves. We also boiled rice, opened a tin of corned beef and Nestlé's cream. It tasted like a banquet after a day afloat.

As the river got wider, the boat got slower; time too slackened its pace. We made an unscheduled stop. Fig, carrying his rifle and with Julio following, beckoned us to follow them. They were hunting for monkeys, Gaucho said. Twenty minutes into the jungle, Fig and Julio were out of sight. So was Gaucho, smashing at everything that didn't stand in his way. So, for that matter, were Peter and Ian. I was left quite cut off from them. I knew I was lost; without a guide, I could never find my way out.

Distances, direction and the depth of the jungle covering made me realise the danger I was in and heightened my fear. I could no longer look at what was interesting or strange. Fear took over. I thought of nothing but possible ways in which I might be saved and was aware of nothing but the maddening mosquitoes and the emptiness filled only with croaks and hollow calls. Above, my only contact with familiarity, broken up and largely obscured patches of blue making shapes 200 feet above my head.

At that instant a soft whistle from Fig further up beckoned us to follow. Instantly the fear evaporated, as we took to our heels trying to imitate their stealth as hunters. Shots rang out, heads craned upwards; I could make out the brilliant red fur mingling with the silver branches.

Ian began blasting with the .38 which we then passed

round like a biscuit tin. There were at least five monkeys, all now perfectly visible and audible in their majestic flight, raining their business down on us as their only defence.

Julio climbed a bank with Ian. Another shot, and I saw a heavy load crash through some air. Julio went to get it. It lay at our feet, its body no longer able to obey its mercury-quick impulses. It gulped air with pathetic need. Glazed and steady, its eyes were terribly human.

We brought the monkey to the river bank, where Figueredu killed it. Turning it on its back we saw the pale grey body of a female monkey. After that was over, we were on our feet again with our guides. I felt relief and thanked God with a feeling that life is held in hands which can let you slip and fall at any time.

After more rapids the monkey was cooked and eaten on a huge fallen tree (but not by me!). Now the hills were behind us we began to be stung by the mariconi, a small fly that lands on your hands and feet and raises a small blood spot, making ankles, wrists and hands blotchy and puffy. But the wounds were displayed proudly and compared with everyone else's. Peter won with 116 bites on his left hand. I was furious I had left the repellent in my haversack in one of the plastic bags.

Our *balseros* were anxious to get to Rurrenabaque, so after a swim – braving the possibility of piranhas – we pressed on and in misty rain reached there, five days after leaving the mining camp. The rest of the trip was more introspective but still full of incident. Because I felt the pressure of time to be back in London to start preparing for *The Performance*, we stuck to the river as far as Pôrto Velho, 1,000 miles from Manaus, and then flew from there.

On the way we travelled by open rowing-boat with a faulty outboard motor and an ancient two-tier river craft like a house-boat. Our experiences were mostly concerned with how to get to the next place. We didn't do the cross-country nature trips, alligator hunting or Amazon river-steamer trip that we had planned. But I did read *The Razor's Edge* and thought about how I shouldn't let other people get their kicks for me; and of the danger on the hunting trip, and the hero of Maugham's novel, Larry, which made me wonder why my life mattered so much to me and where one could make real spiritual discoveries.

We reached the object of our journey on the river of rivers, two miles wide at this point and still 1,000 miles from the sea — Manaus, the old colonial rubber-rich capital of the Amazon — and found rooms at the Hotel Lord.

We had started out from La Paz on April 6th and it was now May 11th. We still had a long way to go to get out of the Amazon, but we managed to buy a lift aboard an old DC6 cargo plane, flying up to Columbia and on to Panama, where I promised to look up a friend, Luis Martinez. We made it and tasted civilisation again in Mrs Martinez's house.

Luis had had to leave as there was a suggestion of his involvement in a revolutionary coup in Panama. I left Peter there — dirty white jeans, open shirt and tennies, sniffing out the action. Ian went back to Australia and his farm, and Gaucho had headed back to La Paz from Rurrenabaque.

Mrs Martinez gave me some money to get up to New York to see Luis, and I called Amanda in LA to tell her to meet me there. I was longing to share my experiences. My friends were a welcome sight and I stayed a week, but Amanda and I were not going to make it.

I left for London where I was greeted with relief and warmth, forgiven, I felt, if not by the film company, then at least by my family. All of them were willing to listen to my adventures, which I tried to make more interesting by editing my small film into a twenty-minute home movie.

I eagerly looked forward to starting work on *Performance*, the new title, which was now ready for filming.

9

PERFORMANCE

In the BBC film entitled *Escape to Fulfilment*, made in 1971, about my religious conversion, the critic and journalist Alexander Walker said: "Some people say Christianity is James Fox's best part to date." Well, I disagree with him – I think *Performance* was, and is, to date.

He also said that in the film *The Servant* I was "like a piece of upper-class porcelain, which would fall apart in one's hand if one held it too firmly". He's right in a way about that. But Chas, the character I played in *Performance*, was not like that. He was a hard nut.

Maybe that was a reason why I was attracted to Chas. I wanted to extend my range and Donald Cammell had written a part in which to do it. By the time I got to London, Donald had Warner Brothers' backing, a producer, Sandy Lieberson, and a co-director, Nick Roeg.

Having two directors was an unusual step, but they complemented each other from the technical and creative standpoint. What was more important, they were in unison about the film's ideas. Exactly what these are is still debated. I saw it then as a film about two archetypal sixties figures – the gangster and the rock star – and their confrontation; others have said it was about schizophrenia and violence.

We were almost semi-documentary in our approach to the South London underworld life and authentic in many of the details of a certain sort of pop star's life. The performers – Turner (Mick Jagger) and Chas (me) – could never really communicate, although each was an outlaw and each came from a similar background.

The story concerned an expanding South London under

world gang emerging from the small time into a big business and a 'cleaner' image. Its boss is Harry Flowers. He has colleagues and a front man (Chas) to do practical work, collect money, threaten lawyers who sub poena favoured clients, and 'decorate' rival businesses likely for takeover.

Flowers tells Chas not to do a 'certain job of decorating' a small betting shop belonging to a former friend of Chas, Joey Maddox (Anthony Valentine). Chas disobeys, busts up Joey's shop, and Joey in revenge destroys Chas's flat and catches and whips him. Chas, feigning unconsciousness, lunges for a hidden gun and kills Joey.

On the run and an embarrassment to Flowers, he hears of a safe house lived in by a dropped-out rock star, Turner (Mick Jagger). He tries to con his way past Turner's mistress, Pherber (Anita Pallenberg), as a juggler. They know he is a criminal on the run but try to help him with a passport photo and medical attention to his back.

Turner also recognises him as an archetypal performer like himself, outside the law, outside society, an assassin. Turner, who has lost his power, his demon, wants to find out Chas's secret, and drugs him to try to see inside him. Chas hates drop-outs and druggers, and rejects this experiment, but spends the night with Turner's other girlfriend (Michelle Breton). The gang find Chas and want to take him away quietly. Turner asks to come too. Chas shoots him.

The film is in two parts: the West End and Chas's domain: and Notting Hill Gate and Turner's flat. For the South London character I had to fill an empty cupboard in my experience. As technical adviser, Donald had got David Litvinoff to make some contacts, the most rewarding of which were through Tommy Gibbons, the then owner of the Thomas à Becket in the Old Kent Road.

There we met Johnny Shannon, who though he was by trade a fruit seller in Berwick Street market and a boxing trainer, 'looked the part' of Harry Flowers. John had no acting experience, but I persuaded the producers to try him, and he played it.

As is quite well known, Tommy was a champion boxer

and promoter and the Becket is used as a gym as well as a pub. It was an excellent place to chat over a drink or a bit of training and get the feel. I also visited some other characters, some of whom had been detained at Her Majesty's Pleasure, and they were all unstintingly helpful.

David was the greatest chat artist in London and could keep an assembled gathering of the unshockable in stitches for hours with his bravura performance, insults and spicy gossip. He also had a gift for showing kindness and, though apparently quite broke, would press an LP or some other gift on you. I had known him since Cy Laurie days.

As I knew Mick quite well already there were no initial nerves or impressions to overcome, but there were other adjustments. I had to become a complete hood, someone who, to the drop-out society of the late 1960s, was a museum piece, using violence in an age of love, becoming a businessman in an age of laughing at the system.

As a character Chas was anathema to Turner, and as I got into the part some of this rubbed off between Mick and myself. For example, he and Anita would tease me with love play while I sat waiting to film in the house in Lowndes Square, or when it came to the interview scene between Turner and Chas, Mick would offer me a drag of a joint.

I would hesitate and he would say: "Trying to give them up, are you?" or something like that. Whereas previously, Mick and I had shared some ironical attitudes, now he in his character became harder, more cynical, more isolated. I believe his performance as Turner was thoughtfully constructed and that it is too little acknowledged for the piece of acting it was.

I decided to spend a week alone in a room in a hotel in Brixton, get a typical haircut and wear nothing but Cecil Gee clothes. Nick Roeg said: "Go away and come back as Chas." I only spent a night at the hotel, but I spent a lot of time at the Becket, with Johnny and Tommy and Beryl his girlfriend, as well as in the gym and at the boxing venues at the Royal Garden Hotel.

By this time I was definitely looking the part. I became

almost completely taken over by the role. I spoke, thought and ate like Chas. It even affected my choice of girlfriend: Donald had cast Ann Sidney, who had been a recent Miss World, as my girl in the film, and we went out for a bit.

Through the writer Francis Wyndham I met Ronald Kray. On tape I listened to recollections of an actual revenge killing by the person involved whose name was not disclosed. It was the time of the Krays, the Richardsons and the growth of crimes using hand guns. We were trying to capture this scene.

If an actor can fill his mind with as much knowledge as possible about a part, it will help him to understand how his character would react, respond and feel in any situation. The rest is communicating it. I think Donald cast me in *Performance* because he felt I had some aggressive instincts in my character, as well as being an actor who responds to directors' ideas and suggestions.

The film was shot entirely on location in the West End, where Chas operated as a front man for an underworld racket. For Harry Flowers' office we used a first-floor suite in Wardour Street, below Shaftesbury Avenue. The day Mick came to film his song there was a highlight. With his hair pinned up and a business suit on, sitting behind a desk, miming to the playback, it was one of those completely successful gambles – a rock and roll song in a different character in the middle of an ultra-realistic setting. Ten years later the music for the film is still strong and highly relevant. Many of the musicians of 1969 who made it are now world famous, among them Ry Cooder.

The fight scene in Chas's flat was not stage managed. Tony Valentine and his two mates held back their punches, but we threw ourselves around in a room somewhere with spectators hanging from the walls to see it. Donald has said great chunks of the fight were cut. Regarding the criticism of violence, it's difficult to judge whether a thing is violent when you're in it, because as a participant the action seems merely technical.

We were choreographing it as a work of art: the re-creation of pain, humiliation, love, pride, revenge, weakness, ruthlessness – what you get when you see it without these references, I cannot judge. When I saw it I had to shut my eyes as Chas raised his gun towards his former friend.

In contrast to this violence was the house in Notting Hill Gate where Turner lived in his *ménage à trois*. This is where the talents of Christopher Gibbs and Deborah Dixon were used to create the pop star's private world, the bedroom adorned with canopies and furs and soft materials, the bathroom and dressing room in Moroccan mosaics and filled with racks of clothes, the main room stacked with amplifiers and equipment, hung with mirrors and partitioned with screens.

There is a telling moment in the film when Turner comes to interview Chas. It is about ten in the morning; he comes into the room. "You can't stay here, Mr . . ." – he goes to the curtains which are slightly apart and very deliberately closes them, turning day to night, turning everything around – "TURNER."

The film's sexual content reflected the times and my own previous experiences – the idea that one could find gentleness and friendship through sex, that sex was not a macho aggressive rugby-club knock. The conventional identity attitudes, that the film makers believed, were more cultural and inherited than truthful. I was sympathetic to those ideas in 1969, although their consequences were by then producing pain and confusion in my life and the lives of my close friends.

I think it was almost impossible for Mick to portray someone who had lost his talent as a performer of songs. After all, in the following year he gave his Hyde Park performance. As far as his search for identity was concerned, I disagreed with Donald and Nick at the time about the ending. Could Turner and Pherber really have believed that they could discover the source of the mystery of Chas's personality and talent by dressing him up as an Arabian assassin and feeding him fly-agaric mushrooms? If they did think that, then I felt that made the character a bit naive.

Because of this slight disagreement I found the last few weeks of the film less enjoyable, but we finished more or less on schedule and all of us felt it had been a great experience. Nick Roeg believed we had something extraordinary and in my bones I felt it, too. The effect the film had on me was really to turn me from drugs as a means of self-discovery and spiritual discovery and from the free and uninhibited use of sex as a means of seeking permanent happiness.

I don't mean to say that I rejected sex, but just the way I had been using it. Cutting myself away from these things left a vacuum, especially by separating me from the friends I enjoyed. The film and the part of Chas had already contributed to that.

What did I replace them with? I returned to all my roots and early childhood friends, like the Burges family who were a couple with four lovely daughters and a farmhouse in Kent. I also turned toward my childhood religion, the Church of England, and would go to church while staying with friends, or on a weekend on my own in London.

A curate in Wandsworth paid me a visit after I had been to Communion a few times and we talked, but only in a general way. I had bought myself a New English Bible New Testament and was reading the odd chapter every now and again. But it still seemed a bit remote from my life.

Performance was edited but no release date was promised. Warner Brothers apparently had doubts about the violence and whether the film was really commercial. I was disappointed.

My friend Rikki Huston had been killed in a car accident but with the help of Christine Burges and a friend, Mary Villiers, I pressed on with decorating 3 Spencer Park. I worked mainly in the garden, which I enjoyed, helped by a local man, Mr Forster.

Through Christine I met Laurence Irving, the grandson of the famous Victorian actor, and paid him several visits. He it was who began to stimulate my interest in the theatre and to cause me to wonder whether I should not try to gain experience and develop my talent on the stage.

Two films were in line for me to do – the first *Biggles*, which John Heyman was producing for Universal, the second Carl Foreman's early life of Winston Churchill. But nothing materialised in 1969, so I enjoyed myself buying a few of Laurence's delightful land and seascapes, a couple of Max Beerbohm's cartoons and some Gordon Craigs.

Eventually I decided to take the plunge on the stage and agreed to do *Henry V* at Bath in the summer. My performance was not quite up to it. I think I was best in the scene with the Princess of France at the end. A friend said she felt I lacked the necessary spiritual quality for speeches like "Oh God of battles, steel my soldiers' hearts . . ." But I did not consider it a wasted effort, and enjoyed the company.

Licking my wounds, I thought I should work harder away from the limelight. An offer to join the Glasgow Citizens' Company under Giles Havergal seemed the most beneficial choice. Meanwhile, for some then unknown reason, I accepted a two-week engagement at the Winter Gardens Theatre in Blackpool over Christmas and the New Year to play Doctor Sparrow in *Doctor in the House*.

10

CONVERSION

Blackpool over the Christmas holiday period becomes full of Scotsmen fleeing south – I suspected, to find somewhere open. Not many of them were lured into the cavernous Winter Gardens Theatre where our little company struggled with poor audiences in a rather lacklustre production. I have scarcely any recollection of trying to perform Dirk Bogarde's famous Doctor Simon Sparrow, a part one is supposed not to be able to fail in, but I think I may have proved otherwise.

We gathered together in some wintry hotel for a company Christmas lunch, but I did not even have the inclination for fun off the stage. I found a modestly pleasant hotel on the front, the Fernleigh, and was given a top-floor bedroom at the side from which I could see the sea and the tower. I felt somehow content, alone and roughing it in traditional theatrical style.

The television lounge was full, but thankfully the noises didn't penetrate upstairs. In the dining room I was given my own table. We had two performances on Christmas Eve, Christmas Day was free, but we had two more on Boxing Day.

On Christmas Day I'd agreed to go to the company lunch and also planned to go to church in the morning and to listen to the Bach Christmas Oratorio on the wireless in the afternoon.

I found the central Anglican church near the theatre and was looking forward to the Christmas story and hymns. Instead of a sermon from the Bible, the preacher told a story. It was about a fourth Wise Man who had not travelled with the other three, following the star, so had arrived too late for the birth of the Saviour, and instead came in time for His death.

I couldn't quite see the point of the story, which only served to make me cynical. How could a minister tell a make-believe story on Christmas Day? I was much happier with the exalted singing of the Bach on the radio. I also began to sketch the view from the bedroom window and the rest of Christmas Day was passed peacefully telephoning my family and the Burgeses and enjoying my Christmas presents which I'd brought with me.

The following morning, I had a rehearsal at 11.30, so I went down to breakfast at about 9 a.m., but this time my table was occupied by a young man, already eating.

I studied the menu. He continued eating. I ordered, our eyes met, he blinked at me through thick-rimmed glasses.

"Hello, I'm Bernie Marks," he said.

We began chatting in a friendly way and I asked him what he was doing in Blackpool. "I've come to spend a day with the Lord," he replied.

He seemed perfectly serious about this and it never entered my head to disbelieve him. He questioned me: "Have you ever thought about Christianity?"

"Oh yes," I said. "I've been thinking about it a lot. I went to church yesterday – a lot of old nonsense! About six months ago I bought a New Testament to read. I think a lot about it."

"What would you say a Christian is?" he asked.

"A Christian is a person who does good to others where he can, follows the teachings of Christ, and . . . that's about it," I replied.

Bernie Marks paused. "Would you like to see what the Bible says a Christian is?" he asked courteously.

"Certainly – yes – very much."

"Would you mind reading this verse out?" he asked. It was a small pocket Bible and he turned it open at Paul's letter to the Romans.

He put his finger on an underlined verse in chapter 3:

" 'Since all have sinned and fall short of the glory of God,' " I read.

"So, are there any natural born Christians, according to this verse?" he queried.

"It doesn't seem so," I must have answered. "That's very interesting."

I had bought my New Testament in order to get first-hand what the Bible said about Christ, and here we were discussing what we thought about this book.

"I think it's true," I said. "I've never met a person who hasn't sinned. I'm sure no one has ever lived who hasn't sinned. Human experience bears that out."

"So you would agree with the Bible?" he said.

"Obviously."

He got out a biro, and drawing on a table napkin he set down his statement on it. I realised I did not even know the basic facts of the Gospel. According to my understanding at the time it would have gone like this: being confirmed meant you were a Christian and going to church was the way of keeping it up.

Bernie showed me objective Bible statements and we discussed and questioned their relevance and truth. There were some areas we agreed you could not prove – for example, the statement in the same book (chapter 6, verse 23): 'The wages of sin is death.' We decided that wages were a way of saying a payment for one's work, so what payment did the work of sin receive?

Well, yes, we were all going to die – that was a fact – and Bernie added this could also mean spiritual death. I didn't understand this completely but agreed the Bible could be saying to those reading it that sin causes spiritual death.

The coffee cups kept being refilled, the paper napkin was becoming quite an illustration and I was following his presentation with interest. The dining room was now empty. Bernie also told me he had come to Blackpool to think. I asked him what about and he said he had come to think about his first four years as a Christian, a state he had resisted for a long time but one to which he was now fully committed. He told me of his happiness at this and how he had come to Blackpool to be quiet after this great change in his life.

He was sensing that I was receptive to his state of mind and began to talk to me about what had brought about this change, about the transformation in his sister's life from a similar conversion, and what Jesus Christ coming into his own life had done. We talked for another hour; he developed the presentation and each point and Bible reference received attention.

Nowhere did I find myself disagreeing or resenting this way of talking about religion. The Bible references almost seemed like a third party guiding our discussion.

It was time to go to rehearsal, so I asked Bernie if he would like to come too. He was eager, as he told me he was a producer of amateur plays and if he hadn't chosen to spend most of his time on Christian work (apart from earning his living, which he did by designing for a mail-order catalogue) he would like to have been an actor.

After the rehearsal we had lunch, and after the performance in the evening he came to the theatre. We had a meal and talked some more. I was discovering behind the familiar facts of Jesus' life a significance which had fresh meaning for me.

We must have discussed a dozen or more subjects, including what the Bible says is the point to life, and what is the meaning of the death of Jesus Christ.

Christ to me then was a superman, beyond human identification, possessing supernatural powers, remote and ideal, but in no way alive now or personally relevant to me or my rather messed-up life. Bernie was communicating a different Jesus. His own confidence at having Him near must have shone out, but it was more than that. As the Gospel story unfolded it became increasingly full of meaning.

On the one hand, here was an actual problem: my sin, spiritual lifelessness or whatever you want to call it. On the other hand, here were all those ways by which I tried to earn some good points with God: going to church, not harming other people, trying to do my best. But I saw that the Bible did not accept this as a way of becoming a Christian. For 'it is by grace you have been saved, through faith. And this is not your own doing – it is the gift of God, not of works lest anyone should boast.'

In a way this was rather reassuring because it was totally different from what one expected. Instead of saying: 'You are guilty. Do better,' it assumed one was guilty and needed to be saved from the penalty of it. This made the death of Jesus Christ anything but remote from my need. He had taken the guilt of my sin for me, and becoming a Christian meant to accept, by faith, His death for me, as a pardon, and to turn away from evil to God for a new spiritual life.

Goodness knows how many times I had said the Creed, sung the carols, taken Communion and listened to the first and second lessons, not to mention the numerous but mostly forgettable sermons.

Bernie and I met for breakfast the following day as he was returning to Manchester and he left me a book by Michael Green, *Runaway World*, and a small tract. He told me if I felt like becoming a Christian I should let him know and he would send me some more books.

He left me and I spent the day, apart from the two shows, thinking about it all. Then, and during the two days which followed, as I walked up and down the promenade and thought and thought about life and death and becoming a Christian, three visual images helped to open my eyes to the relevance of the Crucifixion: the pier, the war memorial and the Blackpool Tower.

I wrote about it in a letter to Laurence Irving from Blackpool on December 28th, 1969:

I think I have found in Blackpool that life can be so much richer if you understand what part God has to play in it – the greatest part. And that to have opened the door and asked Jesus to sup with you is to let into your soul the light, the truth and the beauty of life.

I have begun to understand that life is a wonderful gift of love from God, and that Jesus destroyed the fact of death by His resurrection; that death is only an end to suffering and sin and not to life, which is for ever.

From my bedroom window I have a panoramic view of Blackpool facing south, but it wasn't until I had walked up the esplanade and turned and was walking back towards this same view but at just above sea level, that I saw what struck me as a rather symbolic arrangement of objects.

Three-quarters of a mile down the long straight concrete path, bordered by a sea wall on one side and row upon row of empty benches on the other, rose a tall obelisk to the memory of the dead of two wars. And at right angles to it, stretching to my right out to sea, the North Pier. Behind the obelisk, further down the beach, rose the iron frame of the Blackpool Tower. The scene was lit by a low weak sun as it shone from behind the long projection of the pier and cast a sulphurous sheen across its length toward me.

It was still cold; the sea hardly moved, but the seagulls were displaying beautiful aerobatic tricks as they looped and banked and soared and landed around me as I walked.

Did I not see there man's creation: his fine tower, proof of his technological and aesthetic skill, and his pier, which was a way out and a way back, a rather silly extension of the land in search of happiness and fun above the waves? And did not the sixty-odd feet of clean indestructibly hard Lancashire granite that marked man's self-destructive mania, prove that I must stop and think?

I wanted to tell you all this because I know that you understand what I felt and wanted to share it with you, because I know that you too had been compelled to record your happiness at the gift of life and nature, and your belief that all our sins can be forgiven if we take the step through Jesus.

Looking back after twelve years to those objects on the Blackpool front I think what I was saying was that this life alone is not all there is, and that my achievements, whatever they would be as an actor, could never be the only reason for my existence. Like the tower, they were prominent to me and could give pleasure to others, but were limited.

The pier was the symbol of the fleeting pleasures of sin, the fulfilment I had sought through flights of fantasy. But the search had always led me back to reality again. And the war memorial caused me for the first time to be thankful for the sacrifice of others that I might live and grow up in a free country and choose my destiny. It showed me the cost it had been to others, of their very lives for my sake.

Then I thought about Jesus' death, at such great cost, and for me. Could I refuse His offer of pardon? Like the soldiers' blood-bought freedom, could I ignore the responsibility imposed on me? But for what purpose had He done this? I did not know, but a life which was that significant to God must have purpose.

I went back to my hotel. It was evening now and Bernie had left the day before. He had given me a booklet on what to do to become a Christian if I felt that God was calling to me. To believe was not hard; the facts were offered to me in honest and simple truths by eye-witnesses that compelled trust. But to turn was harder. There was the risk of losing something, of surrendering my legitimate control over my own life, of yielding up my liberty. There was the challenge to change my way of life, my attitude to right and wrong.

What about my money? Who would I be meant to marry? Would I have to become a missionary? These sorts of questions, which in all honesty I had to be willing to have answered by the sovereign choice of God Himself, were harder.

But what my eyes fell upon, as I reflected on the literature Bernie had left me, was this verse: 'But God shows His love for us in that while we were yet sinners, Christ died for us.' Didn't I dare to risk losing something of this life? Did this loss compare with Jesus, who gave up all, His whole life, that I might be given life? Couldn't I trust Him with all my future? If not, who could I trust?

That night I knelt down beside my hotel bed in simple response to a promise of Jesus quoted in the Book of Revelation: 'Behold I stand at the door and knock; if any one hears my voice and opens the door, I will come in to him, and eat with him, and he with me.'

I responded to God in prayer: "I thank You that You promise to come into my life if I ask. And that Jesus died and rose again, so that He could. I ask You to forgive my sins and I open the door of my heart to You. Please come in and help me to live for You."

And He came in, as He promised.

11

STRENGTHENED IN THE FAITH

True to his word, Bernie sent me some literature when he received my postcard that I had invited Christ into my life. Most interesting to me was a little booklet called *Beginning with Christ*, with four 2½ by 1½ inch cards in a little backflap. On them were printed individual Bible verses.

The first, entitled *Assurance of Salvation*, had the reference 1 John 5: 11, 12, and said: 'And this is the testimony, that God gave us eternal life, and this life is in his Son. He who has the Son has life; he who has not the Son of God has not life.'

This verse both confirmed my experience and was a great comfort. The writer of the little booklet urged the recipient to learn this and the three other verses, saying they would be God's means of speaking to and strengthening me in my early days as a Christian.

The booklet was printed by the Navigators, the group Bernie said he had been helped by in Manchester. As Manchester was nearby I decided to go and visit Bernie for the day on my journey to London after the play's two-week run. He met me at the station and seemed to be very happy to see me enjoying my new faith. He said we'd be having a meal at an American missionary family's house and would be meeting some of his friends.

We went to an outlying part of Manchester – with semi-detached houses and small front gardens – where Jack and Joanne Blanch lived. They had two children, and Joanne was expecting another. Bernie introduced me to his two friends – another Bernie Dodd, a physicist, and Ron Finlay, a draughtsman.

We sat down to lunch after thanking God for the food. The Blanches were polite and quite reserved. The food was American style but plain, and the company was warm. Although I felt strange being with altogether more conventional people than I was used to, the thing we had in common, which emerged very quickly, was a love for Christ and an appreciation of the Bible.

I had already felt this delight in reading the Scriptures on my own. Now, with these more mature Christians, and later on my way back to London with Ron, who was going south as well, there was the added pleasure of listening to another person's experience and knowledge of the Bible.

In fact, the journey to London on a Sunday lasted a long six hours, and we spent much of the time with our Bibles open on our knees, enjoying the facts which confirmed all the recent events. I had been through. It seemed my experience in the twentieth century in England was precisely the same as that of believers in the first century in Israel or Greece.

I said goodbye to Ron at Euston feeling that, like Bernie, he had become a friend for life. He gave me the address of another friend to look up – a businessman in Lloyd's insurance, whose name was James Broad. I went back to Spencer Park feeling lighter and calmer than before. I had three weeks before my engagement at Glasgow Citizens was due to start, so I arranged to meet James that Tuesday. He suggested we meet at a church in the City which had a lunchtime service, St Helen's.

I was astonished at this gathering. There must have been 400 or 500 people hurrying into the building and filling up the chairs as well as pews in a semi-circle around the pulpit. For a brief twenty minutes the vicar, the Rev Dick Lucas, expounded the Scriptures in a forthright and convincing manner. The whole company heard him in rapt silence and then joined him in a short prayer. The meeting was followed by a quick cheese and biscuits and coffee at tables laid out behind the seats, before the company made their way back to their offices.

It was very businesslike religion indeed, and I liked it. I

very quickly responded to James' friendship and spiritual life as well. He sometimes came to my house to pray and read a short Bible passage together before the start of the day, or I would meet him for lunch in the City. He was living with half a dozen other Lloyd's insurance men at a house in Wimbledon. A couple called Mike and Susie King rented it, and they were helping these young men grow in their Christian faith.

Like the home in Manchester, it was the centre of a Navigator ministry to business and working people. I learned that the Navigators were an organisation whose purpose was to know Christ and to make him known. I was satisfied that the group was not a cult or separate church, because of the lives of the people I'd met, because of their obviously strong relationship with a church like St Helen's, and because they promoted Christianity only in accordance with the Bible.

But my family and friends were not so sure. My parents were understandably sceptical of my sudden conversion and of the connection with an American organisation. In my enthusiasm I laid my exciting discoveries on them with a heavy hand and their reaction was: 'Don't try and convert us!'

What was probably even harder to take was that my new awareness of spiritual life had for the time being obscured all other considerations, and I fear I was either too self righteous or too other-worldly for them at first. Having found an explanation for many hitherto perplexing uncertainties I became dogmatic and paradoxically rather uncaring. I became extremely wary about my former interests and relationships. For instance I broke up an affair with an old friend by writing a rather insensitive letter. I sorted through all my LPs that had associations with my sexual relationships and gave them away. When I visited an old friend who showed me some photographs of some very young nude girls, I was shocked.

I could only interpret my Christianity in terms of a new life, a new beginning, and associated some former things with what was now dead or passed. I felt it was better to separate myself from these old associations and get involved with new relationships among the Navigator group, who were mostly young businessmen and students. I also had to separate myself physically from London to go and begin my contract in Glasgow.

My brother Edward had been at the Citizens Theatre and was well known there. His stories of happy experiences in the repertory there encouraged me. I was pleased to be going to work with Giles Havergal who had been at Harrow at the same time as myself.

My first part was Hector in *Heartbreak House* which I enjoyed. The second play was an adaptation of R. L. Stevenson's *Ebb Tide*, a story about a British writer in the South Pacific who is shipwrecked with some drunken cronies. It was a modern parable I should have been able to understand and portray, but I couldn't.

There then followed two more plays which I was meant to be in. An Anouilh play, I think it was *Time Remembered* and *The Balcony* by Jean Genet. Just before the opening of the Anouilh they called an unexpected rehearsal on a Sunday. I had already informed them that I had been invited to a Navigator conference that day. I was told I was needed to rehearse and I had to decide where my commitment lay. I went to the conference. When I got back, Giles called me into his office and after alleging that my Christianity was interfering with my acting he gave me the sack. It was really true that I was not able to separate my faith from getting on with the job and unfortunately we never got around to talking about it before the crunch came. At the time I felt I was being persecuted.

While all this was going on I had found a church I liked very much, St George's Tron, and I was received very warmly. The minister George Duncan was an inspiring Bible teacher and became a friend.

My mother came to visit me in Glasgow and brought me a biography of Dietrich Bonhoeffer, the German theologian. She too found it hard to separate my Christianity from 'the

William we used to know'. She was quite offended when she asked George Duncan what he saw as the answer to one of her friends' children's drug problems and he replied, "Jesus Christ is the only answer".

Perplexed by my experiences, I returned to London. My father decided he needed to caution me. "You can't be an actor and a fully dedicated Christian. You know that being an actor is not a nine-to-five job, but requires your whole dedication when you are working." I felt in a dilemma — the two worlds seemed to oppose each other.

Back in London I concentrated on gardening at my house and used to go in to the City to St Helen's, or to a Navigator meeting of businessmen after work. There I met Roger, an American.

I began to wonder about living alone in my six-bedroomed house, so I moved into the house in Wimbledon with the others. I wondered whether I ought to give my house to God's work or the money from the sale of it.

It was summer and at this moment, my father, who had been complaining for some time of not feeling one hundred per cent, went for an X-ray and medical and was found to have lung cancer. An immediate operation was called for. He was taken to Midhurst. They operated and closed him again — the cancer was found to be too widespread for surgery. My father was only fifty-seven, and this was a deep shock. We already knew that he was a stupendously brave man. All of us gathered round him knowing that he had only months to live. My friend Roger Anderson, and Dotty his wife, invited me to live with them in this time of confusion and grief.

I willingly accepted, feeling helpless, knowing in my heart the comfort and peace of my faith, and desperately wanting to share it, yet recognising that my expression of Christianity had little apparent comfort for others.

At the same time *Performance* came out and got some excellent reviews. I did not know how to take it. I had to continue my acting career, but what should I do?

For the eight hundredth anniversary of Thomas à Becket's

martyrdom E. Martin-Browne was directing *Murder in the Cathedral* in Canterbury Cathedral. He offered me two small parts, a tempter and a knight. I accepted. By doing an essentially religious play, I wondered if I would be more successful in combining Christianity with acting. I only succeeded in becoming more frustrated. I wasn't exercising my talents in what I could do best and I found that Christian drama isn't necessarily an aid to Christian development or even communication.

It was also a time of spiritual confusion. I was drawn into some teaching to do with certain experiences and gifts of the Holy Spirit and got into a big argument with one Christian lady about this. Things became very heated, but what brought me round to realising that I was being rather opinionated about this subject was that the lady's husband did not try to put me right, although he knew much more than I did, but instead he treated me gently and listened sincerely to my views and came up with a suggestion that we should look at the whole thing together.

Despite having separated myself from a lot of my old friends one of them did not stand afar off in my early days as a Christian. Johnny Shannon sought me out in Wimbledon, and we went for a drink. Thinking I'd been brainwashed or kidnapped by some religious cult for my money, he told me: "If you want me to thump them for you, Jim, I will."

I tried again in the theatre as Captain Jack Absolute in *The Rivals* in Canterbury. It was the last play I was to do. My father was becoming more ill, and Edward had been looking into the claims of a German doctor, Josef Issels, who was apparently having some success with incurable cancer.

Against British medical advice we took Pa to Germany and he underwent some dreadful therapy to try to shrink the tumour. He fought for his life but his condition only grew worse. He was brought home early in the New Year and for his final few weeks he was at his home in Cuckfield, with my mother, his family and friends. I know he was glad to be there. On January 21st 1971 he died peacefully.

The shock to us all, and especially my mother, was of course terrible, but I continued to feel an outsider to them and his death robbed me of a father I loved and of his wise advice.

Then an unexpected comfort came in the form of a challenge from a Navigator leader, Robb Powrie-Smith. "Do you think you could go to Guildford University and start a Navigator work?" he asked.

I knew very well what he was implying. To begin a work from scratch at a university entailed doing effective personal evangelism among students to bring them to consider and respond to God's invitation to enter his Kingdom. It required a strong grasp of the Scriptures to be able to instruct new believers and faith in prayer to see God bring them to follow him wholeheartedly. Then it required that some of the students were trained up by me to be able to do the same as I'd done! It needed discipline, love and strength of character to hack it out.

I gulped. "Of course not. How could I?"

He searched me with a long pause. "What would it take for you to do that?"

"Time . . . help," I stammered.

"Are you willing to pay that price?" He left my tentative yet eager response without comment.

The challenge was not to be taken up then, but I felt I'd been offered something more demanding and potentially rewarding than any film part that had ever come my way.

In March my friend Roger Anderson was to make a tour to Australia and New Zealand, going by way of Beirut and Singapore, to help Navigator leaders in those countries. He asked me if I'd like to accompany him and tell of my conversion to student audiences and local Christians. I accepted as I'd enjoyed Roger's company so much.

We arrived in Beirut first and spent a few days there. Just as we were leaving for Singapore I had a telegram saying that Carl Foreman the producer wanted to see me in connection with playing young Winston Churchill in the film. But having already set out on this two-month journey I decided that I couldn't turn back.

During the trip I spoke at barbecues, garden parties, student meetings and screenings of my films, at some of which there was noisy opposition. I even appeared in a Kung Fu stage production arranged by the Navigator group in Singapore and felt acutely embarrassed. I think the heckling and opposition at times only strengthened me. Why did people react to Christianity with more emotion than objectivity?

I came back through the USA, stopping off in Los Angeles to try to see some old friends and invite them to a dinner where I could give them an account of my Christian conversion. Some came and others gave me the cold shoulder. I didn't know whether to get in touch with Amanda, who I wanted to see and yet was frightened of facing. I felt a great responsibility to communicate 'spiritual things' to people. It was like inhabiting a different world. When I got back to England I had a clearer idea of what I wanted to do. I had remembered Robb's challenge and had talked to Christians in different countries about the steps they had taken in getting a work going.

The BBC approached me to make a documentary about my conversion in their series *Escape to Fulfilment*. When it was over, I had to decide what to do in the longer term. I had met another Christian, Alan Sims, from near Sheffield, that summer, and we immediately became friends. He was an administrative manager with British Steel at Stocksbridge. He invited me to come north to live with his family. So I decided to take two years away from films and acting altogether and to concentrate on whatever it took to become a Navigator worker.

Robb said that I'd have to get a job while I was up there so I bought a copy of the *Sheffield Morning Telegraph* and sat down in Barkers Pool to study it. Just about the only job I could see that I could do was as a salesman and there was a vacancy for a post with Phonotas, to get new clients for their office telephone sterilising service in the Sheffield and Rotherham area.

I was interviewed in Hillsborough by a Mr Rowley, the area manager. I think he liked the fact that I'd been in the army and seemed unaware that I was a dropped-out actor. I had to work entirely on commission, calculated on the number of telephones obtained for cleaning.

On my first day at work, I went to London Road in Sheffield. My second stop was a car showroom. The manager interviewed me. "You're James Fox, aren't you? What on earth are you doing here?" I told him I wanted him to sign up to have his five phones cleaned weekly and that I'd come to live in Sheffield and was doing this as a job. I was given the contract by the incredulous manager. I worked until five o'clock, made thirteen other calls and got only one more contract. In the first few weeks, I made about twenty-five calls a day, but eighty per cent of these turned out to be refusals. It was often unrewarding and tedious – I would even say masochistic if there'd been any pleasure in it – but it never occurred to me to do anything else! I felt I was doing it to be in work and be toughened up in the real world. As I walked past the steel mills of Attercliffe and Rotherham I looked into the vast workshops that resembled film studio sets and saw the red hot metal being pounded by heavy hammers. I felt I was being slammed and shaped myself.

I toured every business district in Sheffield and in Rotherham, as well as visiting Derby, Doncaster and Barnsley over the next eighteen months. My sales performance improved. Often I was recognised, always with the same disbelief. At other times the manager would carefully avoid asking me why I was working as a salesman. When my figures weren't good enough, Mr Rowley wrote me notes saying things like: 'Leave no stone unturned.' I eventually climbed into the charts of the nation's top twenty Phonotas salesmen. Fame at last!

My family had been taken aback by my move to the north and by my new occupation. They were also amused by my browny green suit and knitted tie. On one visit home my mother said, "You look like a grocery assistant with that haircut!"

In the evenings we would have evangelism visits, meetings and Bible studies or listen to Alan speaking from the Bible to a crowd of about fifty in his own sitting room. My life had never been busier, and all the experiences were new.

I got fed up with working as a salesman and told Robb so when he was staying at Alan's.

'My brethren, count it all joy when you fall into diverse temptations; knowing this, that the trying of your faith worketh patience,' he said quoting slowly and deliberately from his favourite Authorised Version with a rather sly expression on his face.

I did not wish him much joy as I said good night and closed the door behind me. But I respected him.

At first I found it hard to relate to students and I'm sure the feelings were mutual. In a student magazine Alan and I were nicknamed 'Sins and the Grin', and we were described as obsequiously knocking on doors, and applying the thumb-screws. In one of our sketches which we put together when we had a party I decked myself out in a green mac, with a two-foot square Bible, to reconstruct the scene.

In all the adjustments my appreciation for Alan's family grew. I think what I had been looking for all my life was friendship. Being able to talk freely about my hopes and problems to someone who was really interested. This is what I found in the Sims family.

In different ways, too, I saw the quality of the Christian life in others. In February of the following year Doug Sparks' wife, Leila, who was only forty-two, got cancer. Like my father's it spread rapidly. She and Doug had four children, whose ages ranged between eight and sixteen. I marvelled at the inner strength they were given to face the situation, but not without tears and disappointments. Their patience in suffering showed the great strength of meekness and dependence. They accepted these circumstances as it were from God's hand and carried on trusting his perfect goodness with absolute realism. As I reflected on death and suffering and what I was giving my life to, I came back to the conclusion that my Christianity was only Jesus Christ.

The better I got to know him the better I would understand what he wanted me to do.

During the summer of 1972 I met Mary, my future wife, at a garden party at the Sims' home. She looked absolutely gorgeous in a long crimson velvet skirt and white frilly blouse, as summery as a sweet william. Her reputation had preceded her as a theatre sister at St Thomas's Hospital in London and as someone who had helped many nurses in London to follow Christ. I might have been daunted by her reputation, but instead I was captivated.

I lent her my travel books on Italy as she was going there for a holiday before coming up to Sheffield in September. As I got to know her I loved her enjoyment of people, her clear strong mind and her relaxed manner. I pushed our romance but she was more hesitant, having come to Sheffield to lead girls, not to be involved with a man. My reputation as a film star, which gave other girls a thrill, had, she informed me, only made her determined not to get involved. But we did go out together a few times and at Christmas I met her family.

Feeling that I'd exhausted my talents as a salesman for Phonotas, I began to think about another job. Was this the time to make a return to acting? I had a holiday with Doug in Morocco in January, and talked about it also with Mary, as by then we were about to become engaged. I also told my agent to see if there was any interest, but in my heart I knew it was not God's particular timing for me to come back in 1973, so I wondered what else I could do.

I was attracted by the estate agency business as I was interested in people and houses and was interviewed by T. Saxton and Co. They had no vacancies on the house side, but had need for an assistant on the industrial side. I was delighted when they offered me the job.

My first bit of estate work was for Mary and me. Through knocking on doors in our favourite district of Sheffield we found a beautiful Georgian terraced house. We were married in September, after making some hasty preparations to the house before leaving.

While we were on our honeymoon, the Sheffield Navigator group hung our hall, landing and stairs with our chosen wallpaper and put up our bedroom curtains. We arrived back from Greece late at night to find a note, some milk and this super 'welcome home'.

12

A CHRISTIAN FAMILY

We began married life in our first home, found places for my long-stored bits of furniture and pictures, and started to tile the bathroom ourselves while we waited for our kitchen to be completely refitted.

I had some William Morris chrysanthemum wallpaper from Colefax and Fowler which looked charming in our dining room and sent for my old battery lawnmower from Spencer Park which still worked well, to tackle the neglected lawn. I went to the office each day by bus down London Road, which I had walked so many times as a salesman, and in the evening I came home to my wonderful wife and her cooking.

As winter drew on we battled against the darkness brought on by the 'three-day week' of the miners' dispute, doing our work by Calor gas and getting home earlier. Business remained brisk on the house side, but on my industrial and office-letting side it was naturally a bit of slack.

My job at Saxton's was to process work, from helping measure and draw up particulars to circularising them, talking to prospective clients, and informing solicitors in the event of a sale or lease.

One job I was given was to design and construct a display of Saxton's properties for the Yorkshire and Humberside office seminar. I enjoyed this practical creative project. It was only after I left the firm that the partners mentioned their feeling that I ought to be using my talents in the acting world. However it was towards Christian work, not acting, that I was leaning. I very much wanted to join the Navigators' staff and start to work among students.

Leeds University kept coming into my thoughts. At work I handled brochures about the city for our Leeds office. I had a family connection – my great-grandfather founded the Leeds Forge Steel Works. And, most importantly of all, I was aware that the Navigators were not represented at this important university – and wouldn't it be appropriate for Sheffield, another Yorkshire city, to provide the labourers?

Now that God had given me a wife with such capacity and experience, the Navigators were also interested in inviting us to join their staff. I was in a position to support our family financially for the time being through my invested earnings from films. But it would mean selling our house in Sheffield after living in it for only ten and a half months.

The Heath Government fell over the miners' dispute on March 1st. At that moment we were thinking hard about our future. We consulted with friends and waited on God for peace or lack of it and for direction from the Bible. A promise of Jesus encouraged me: "You did not choose me, but I chose you and appointed you that you should go and bear fruit and that your fruit should abide."

After fifteen months, grateful for the experience, I left Saxton's. I was about to change my career again, this time to full-time Christian work. Of course every Christian serves God 'full-time' in one sense, but for us this was a special call, one which brought together a number of experiences and longings, and we responded to it with high idealism and peace of heart.

Steve Covell, who led the Navigators' student work, also planned to move with his family to Leeds to be with us and to make it his base. I began to make trips to Leeds from Sheffield to meet Christians in the halls of residence. On our first afternoon's house-hunting we found a home that we liked, then sold our Sheffield house almost the day that it went on the market. By August we were unloading our things in West Park, near Headingley, and Mary was expecting our first child.

For the start of our first term a group of seven under-graduates from Cambridge University came to help us with our evangelism. We introduced ourselves to 'freshers' in their rooms and asked if they would be interested in discussing Christianity and studying the Bible. Over thirty said they would. During the year we held meetings, and in November, Robb (who had challenged me in 1971: "Could you go to Guildford and start a ministry?") talked to a group of these contacts in our sitting room. Some became Christians that year, but we did not see many of them stay around us for long. We laboured more for our results than for God's glory.

Our son Thomas was born in February of our first year in Leeds, which brought a different set of priorities to bear on our lives. I was slow to respond to this, still thinking that 'doing the job' meant putting other people before my family. In addition I began to struggle with the evangelism, feeling I hadn't the courage to approach strangers with the gospel, and not knowing how to start friendships with students from scratch.

I went out and bought a huge blackboard and easel, on which to draw diagrams and list principles. I was treated tolerantly by our handful of students, who probably prayed that I'd relax a bit more and try to be less of the teacher. I felt that the work was very slow, both in the many conversations I had which often seemed to result in nothing and in the little apparent growth in our lives and those of our group.

My friend Alan had words of common sense. He said that since I was doing the job at my own expense, I was answer-able only to God and to myself. I kept on trying to achieve spiritual results by effort without much success. I should have relied on God to use me despite deficiencies.

By the end of our second year Steve talked to me about my financial situation. Good friends of ours had made regular gifts of money to us since we began but the amount was small in comparison with our regular expenditure. Our money was coming mainly from dividends and the sale of shares and, as Steve said, this was not a bottomless pit.

I was assisting that year at a training programme at the Wycliffe Bible Translators' headquarters near High Wycombe. There were thirty-seven of us, mostly young Christians who were university students. There was a very good spirit. At the end of the programme the leader mentioned that our financial needs were about £400 a monty, but that we were currently receiving only about £50-£75.

We had been involved for nearly two years in this way in Leeds. Now this small group, and others we notified by letter, pledged to give to us regularly. In December we received no less than £500 in one month from this new group of supporters. Our support was sustained with minor fluctuations for the next four years, and we always had enough.

One month after the programme I received a cheque for £10,700 from a previously unsettled business matter in the past (this was seven years after my last film). I believe the explanation for this is that God provided the money we needed through this way. I was more expectant for the evangelism in the autumn of 1976. We surveyed 160 students and found people open to talk, but even more important, in answer to prayer, we were led to people who were spiritually hungry. I had already shown a few people how to become a Christian, but this year I was personally involved in a student's — Paul's — conversion. He had responded to an invitation to talk about the Bible. One evening he came over and wanted to get things sorted out. I explained to him that he needed to receive Christ. He agreed. We talked about what he might say to God and then sitting at our dining-room table he prayed a simple prayer that Christ might come into his life. It was one of the greatest thrills in my life and even greater still to watch him grow as a Christian. By December of that year there were fifteen new Christians and we knew they would go on, for the Bible says: 'He who is of God hears the words of God.' They were people like that.

During that summer, Robin, our second son, was born

and named after my father. Two sons within fourteen months may be a double blessing but it doubled the nappies and everything else as well.

I sometimes became depressed with the responsibility and routine of life as a student leader, husband and father. I wanted to escape from my circumstances. I thought how unsuitable I was for the job I was doing. I was tempted to give it up. But I began to find ways of coping with self pity and negativity. Mary and I talked honestly about how we felt. I prayed about the things that worried me and confided to a few close friends things I'd previously bottled up.

In Jubilee Year the Navigators held a huge congress in Germany over Easter. Committed Christians from all of Europe met together for four days. We took thirty from Leeds by rail to Essen. I have never found big conferences much to my liking, but we live in an age of conferences and it was heartening to see God at work in the lives of people from so many different situations – people with no Christian background from France, Spain and Finland.

As yet there seemed to be more from the sciences, business and nursing than from the arts. Coming back from Essen I wondered why my own world of acting and the arts in general seemed slower to respond to the new life in Christ. I wanted to do something about it myself but still felt that God wanted us where we were.

As we saw it, the chief reasons for staying in Leeds were our involvement with a new supervisor, Dirk van Zuylen, and the chance to help our more promising young disciples achieve their potential as leaders. As usual I needed the exhortation from Scripture to continue: 'Take heed now, the Lord has chosen you to build a house for the sanctuary; be strong and do it.'

Dirk, a Dutchman, supervised three student ministries in the north, including ours. He was from a flower-growing family who were Christians. In his teens he hadn't had much time for religion. At seventeen he barely escaped death in a construction accident. His pastor asked him: "Where would you have been if you had died?" Knowing the answer, he began to think more seriously about becoming a Christian. Soon after, he asked Christ into his life.

From that time he had loved the Word of God and built up several student ministries in Holland and England, but in 1976 he had suffered kidney failure. When we began to work with him, he was on a kidney machine three days a week but still managed to help his team lead the three student ministries.

At the start of the new university year we began a course of lectures on tape for the students by Dick Lucas, the vicar of St Helen's, Bishopsgate, on the book of Romans. Those who showed dedication and ability were delegated work like leading a Bible study or taking some evangelistic initiative in the halls of residence.

Of course we were all inexperienced, but now the process was beginning with a new generation. This made us all the more vulnerable, because these Christians got an even closer look at our lives.

One incident stayed in all our minds. On Saturday mornings we sometimes did odd jobs around our house. This time the gang arrived about ten and were due to clear some rubbish for which I needed the car. I was wearing my work cardigan. People had already arrived and were waiting downstairs when I realised I couldn't find my car keys.

When things are lost, I get seized with panic. I shouted to Mary downstairs: "Have you seen my keys?" She came up and we had a look – no keys.

"I suppose the children have taken them. Thomas! Robin! Have you got my keys?" Two small faces watched me cautiously. "Well, find them . . . go on. Look for them!" Robin scrambled off earnestly and looked in things, and Thomas ran downstairs to get away.

By this time I was in high dudgeon. Charging downstairs I screamed at half a dozen bewildered students: "Don't just stand there – look for them! Go on – properly! Get down on your hands and knees! Use some initiative!"

People melted away before my tracks as I crawled feverishly around. Mary tried to stop the children crying and made suggestions. Rushing upstairs again I heard a familiar rattle from somewhere near. I patted myself. Smugly concealed in my cardigan pocket were the wretched keys.

"I've found them!" I hailed cheerily.

"Oh good – where were they?" Mary sighed.

"In my cardigan . . ."

Students, adept at the deadpan, mumbled and got up off the floor, and I led the relieved troops out through the front door, leaving the wreckage of a ten-minute tornado behind us.

My acting services were now requested by the Billy Graham film company for a small part in *No Longer Alone*, the story of Joan Winmill, an actress who was converted at one of the Billy Graham London crusades. I accepted the two-week engagement as it was possible to fit it into the university vacation. My family were pleased that I was taking a part in a film and it brought us together more closely. But should I follow it with further acting work? As far as I was concerned, it was a one-off part.

The reason for staying in Leeds was now mainly the experience I was gaining with Dirk and his team. We felt sure we should stay for at least another year. Our third boy, Laurence, was born in the summer and with our daughter, Lydia Rose, being born sixteen months later; I was glad to be able to work at home, to be on hand to help.

Wondering what to do next, after six years with students, we turned our eyes towards Italy and the possibility of going there as Navigator workers. I went on a visit with some friends to the north, looked over a university town and talked with students and some local Christians. But it didn't seem to click that God was sending us there.

When it came, guidance for the next step, like the pillar of cloud by day and the column of fire by night for the Israelites, was much more obvious.

13

COMEBACK

The first return I made to acting after the interruption of National Service in the early sixties was as an upper-class type, which reflected my background of Harrow and the Coldstream Guards. What could I offer at the end of the seventies after a lay-off in Christian work? I had already been offered the part of a drop-out monk! One thing that concerned me was that I had lost or buried some of that ego which is necessary if one is to get up in front of a camera or audience. I had loved the limelight as an eleven year old. But now I had put aside some of my self-centredness as being un-Christian. To some extent I may have acted as I thought a Christian should behave but I still had not found a confidence that my mother likes to call 'coming to terms with yourself'.

We had not kept in touch with many old friends from the business and I felt most of them must have decided that I had become a nut. Thanks to the successful films that I had been in and to Edward and Robert's publicity my name was still known to the public, even if it was sometimes mistaken.

My wife and I were sitting in a cinema in Leeds watching *A Bridge Too Far*, a film in which my brother played General Sir Brian Horrocks, and at the end of a particularly fine piece of 'rallying-the-troops' acting by Edward, a man behind me turned to his companion and said, "He's a bloody good actor, that James Fox."

I still got recognised in the street and there had been a steady press interest. My reputation as an actor was still alive. When I went to do a TV interview on *Saturday Night at the Mill* Bob Langley said how much he had liked my performances. As a result of that interview I got some direct advice from my mother, "You'd better lose some weight and stop making those terrible faces. You're just like your brother, you both do it when you get nervous."

By now Edward had made the *Edward and Mrs Simpson* serial and had become famous. People often mentioned that just as I dropped out of the business Eddie's career took off. I'm glad he succeeded so well. Whenever we are together we have a huge laugh, although people like to make something of our rivalry. There isn't much to it. I rather envy his range, and he may have been jealous of my success, but we get on rather well.

He showed brotherly concern over my comeback, suggesting I talked with some of his director friends and get some advice. He invited me to lunch at Wilton's for a chat which turned out to be an amusing occasion.

Lady Di, as she then was, had just been to Sandringham for the weekend. She had cleverly avoided the press by taking a regular train, getting off at a nearby local station and then being picked up by a car and taken to a back door. At our table, Eddie and I replayed the scene as we imagined Prince Charles and his father might have planned it, with imaginary Ordnance Survey maps spread out in front of us and suitably Royal Family accents.

"Take her down past Dicky's lake and cross the B4527."

"Send the decoy Range Rover up past the main gates at 70 m.p.h."

"Stick a gillie's hat down over her ears, nip through the back gate and it'll be all over before the blighters can lick their pencils."

Eddie was in expansive mood, having just returned from India where he'd played a guest part in *Gandhi*. There were no prices on the menu, which rather invited you to throw caution to the wind. He ordered caviar to start. As the guest, I thought I'd better have melon. He continued with grouse; I chose the sole. He finished with a cigar and I settled for a sorbet and coffee. I glanced at the bill when it came. It was over eighty pounds. Eddie blanched a bit. I apologised but he kept cool and paid up. It was a sweet way to say welcome back into the business.

Our arrival in London happened to coincide with my younger brother Robert's venture into management with Robert Fox Productions. We went to his first two plays and were very impressed by his theatrical and business sense. Robert is one of the funniest people I know and very like my father. I am glad to say he and his wife Celestia, who is a casting agent, have always been supporters of my acting. It was through Celestia that the whole subject of *The French Lieutenant's Woman* came up. While I was still in Leeds she had talked to some people who thought I would be good for it. She enquired and found out that I was returning to acting and would be interested in reading it.

I bought the book and liked it, but not unreservedly. Mary and I had already booked a weekend in a London hotel in February to see my agent and get a feel of London again. I was told I could read the script when I got to London. I couldn't wait to open it and as I read it I was not disappointed. Harold Pinter had adapted it brilliantly. The leading male part of Charles was well within my ability. One of America's brightest actresses, Meryl Streep, was cast as the leading female and Karel Reisz was directing, a chance to make up for my contract-breaking on *Isadora*.

You can imagine my dilemma. So much was right. I could see that this film would put me back at the top as a film actor and would be satisfying to make. But there was a hang-up. Several times the characters used 'Jesus' and 'Christ' in normal conversation as expletives. There was a drunken scene in a Victorian brothel with Charles and his friends watching a tableau of posing prostitutes. The leading man and the leading lady, who were both married, were having an affair. There was a strong attack on Victorian religious hypocrisy which may well have been valid but which also derided the faith that it was supposed to represent. And there was a climactic sexual encounter which went all the way in what it showed.

I lay on my hotel bed in the Kensington Close in an acute dilemma. What could be the reason for this wonderful opportunity coming my way if I was only going to have to turn it down. I became depressed at what I had to throw away.

I reread the script. I read bits aloud to Mary. She knew how much I liked it. Pinter provides the best framework for an actor to build a character and convey the reality behind the spoken word, but there was no doubt that there were certain things in it that I could not perform with a clear conscience. For safety I rang a broad-minded Christian friend whom I respected very much and asked him for an opinion. He dropped the script back to the hotel personally.

"I don't see how you could do it, dear James, without offending and confusing other Christians."

I agreed. We felt that this offer must have come as an indication from God that something even better in the film business was going to come my way. This was the only reason we could see for it. It was good that I should still be considered for such a leading part but I would rather not make a quick decision and find myself making a comeback in the wrong vehicle.

I rang Karel. He was friendly and pleased to hear that I was back in acting. He wanted to know what I thought of the script and if we could meet. I stumbled out my praise for the film, my pleasure at being asked to read it and went on, "But there are just too many things that I felt uncomfortable about."

"What things?" he said.

I began with the blasphemies, the brothel, the climax in the Exeter Hotel.

"Oh, well," said Karel. "I see. That's it then. So you're really back in acting?" he asked.

"Yes."

"I'm pleased," he said. "Let's meet."

We hung up.

What happened next in my attempted comeback was even more perplexing. My agent rang me in Leeds with a hint that ATV were going to make a thirteen-part TV serial of *Dan Dare*. You may remember that Dare was the front-page story of the 1950s boys' comic *The Eagle*: a Second World War Battle of Britain ace then engaged in deadly combat in space against the evil ruler of the Universe, a little green man called the Mekon.

Dan was a great hero figure to a generation of present day forty year olds. His appeal to me was that he was ultra-cool in a tight scrape, was always on the side of fair play and could usually end up on top in a scrap with the forces of darkness: most Englishmen's concept of a good bloke and my idea of a juicy part.

The idea of the serial had occurred to Leon Clifton, an American producer who had persuaded ATV to back the project. My agent told me that Clifton and the head of ATV serials would like to meet me. I came down from Leeds by train and was taken to the offices of an international film production company in Mayfair who specialised in making TV commercials. Drinks and dinner were served by an excellent catering service in an impressive conference room with stereo equipment and a long stripped pine table. I was trying my best to give a good showing as their potential Dan. I was given a three-course grilling, and naturally enough I was asked about my reasons for leaving acting and now coming back.

We listened to some music which had already been specially composed for the serial, a brilliant modern arrangement of Chopin on the electric guitar. We discussed the treatment. The script had been written by Phil Redmond, the creator of the TV series *Grange Hill*. His version aimed at abandoning some of Dan's post-war attitudes and bringing his problems into the 1980s. As I read the script in bed, in the luxury flat they put me up in, I knew it was dead right.

I couldn't sleep. This had to be the better way I had hoped for when *The French Lieutenant's Woman* fell through. I'd already given them my answer by my enthusiasm for the project and the way they saw it, so all I had to do was wait for their reaction to me. They were equally keen and I was offered the part the next morning.

Everyone was thrilled. I rang Mary with the news and she was equally overjoyed. I went back to Leeds and negotiations got under way. Finally, after sweating through lots of compromises on both sides, a deal was agreed. Discussion on the other casting and matters to do with the technical problems of producing a space drama on TV were explored. By now I had met Rodney Bewes, who had already been cast as Digby, Dan's batman, and we had hit it off. The first thing Rodney did was to ring his best friend Tom Courtenay and take Tom and his girlfriend, Daphne, his own wife, Mary and me out to a 'welcome-back-to-the-business' dinner.

We were due to start preparing in October in order to begin the studio work in January. The timing was perfect for us as we had time to take our summer holiday near Padstow in Cornwall and still get back to Leeds, pack up, leave and get down to London by October 1st. We did this, but just as we were settling into London the news came that the series was off. Technical difficulties and cost were given as the principal reasons. There was nothing to do but pay off those of us who had already been contracted and shelve it.

It was an awful disappointment. Again I searched for a reason why this series, which seemed to be acceptable in every way, should have fallen through. Apart from the practical reasons I had been given I still don't know why. I had to accept the feeling that one of the best opportunities that British television had had in years had been lost. It certainly was an eventful start to a comeback, and since it threw me out of work just when I expected to be employed for two years I had to find something to do. After all, I had now been back in the profession nearly a year and had nothing on the screen to show for it. It was at that moment that I decided to write this book.

Then along came *The Astors*, a major BBC TV series about the influential political family. Philip Hinchliffe, the producer, had put my name at the top of his list for Waldorf Astor three years before. When he heard I was back he rang my agent. He and Bill Slater, the original director, interviewed me in the bar at the BBC TV Centre in Wood Lane. There were plenty of heads turning in our direction, as there had been at Elstree when I went to the ATV canteen on a Dan Dare visit. In both places I got the heartening feeling that people in the business were saying a genuine 'we're glad you're back'.

Bill and Philip were unanimous and called my agent the same afternoon. They even had a definite starting date and since it was the BBC I felt this one was sure to start on time. A huge pile of scripts and background material dropped through my door and I read the six episodes of the series that involved me with pleasure.

The series called for both Nancy and Waldorf, her husband, to go from their twenties to their seventies. It was an interesting challenge. For the first time I would be playing a married man and a father. The research was made easier by the extraordinary skill and dedication of the make-up, wardrobe and wig people, and also by the vast amount of photographic and written material that was available concerning this well-known family. But the biggest shock was to see what the real Waldorf looked like: he was extremely dark, with striking brown eyes. We decided we had to get as close as possible to a physical likeness so three different wigs were made with three shades of contact lenses to go with them. It was a total transformation.

While all this preparation was going on for my start on *The Astors* in July I had another interview at the BBC. I was rung up one cold, February afternoon by my agent asking me to go over to the Television Centre to be seen by the producer of the *Love Story* series. Jane Asher had already been cast as the wife in a story about a childless couple. Jane and I share the same agent and she had been positive about me for the husband. Of course I knew of her but I hadn't kept up with her theatrical career in the seventies. I was given the play to read in the secretary's office and had time to decide that I liked the idea and the character. Then I was wheeled in.

I was very nervous. Again they said they'd liked my work in the past, and asked why had I come back, and so on. The director Alan Grint talked little and peeped at me through shady glasses. I've always considered two things to be absolutely essential in producing my best work on any project: the script and the director. Alan threw me by his non-communication but I knew that he had a good reputation and felt that I had to take the plunge. After I had read Paula Milne's script I was reassured. Again the producer rang the same day to say they wanted me. Apparently my nervousness had worked in my favour as they felt it was right for the character that he should be uptight.

For any BBC play or serial you have to meet together for the first time to read through the whole script with all the actors and the production people present. Our first read-through was at a church hall near Holland Park. I was called on to sing several Lennon and McCartney songs and unfortunately the very first sounds in the play were my singing this beautiful, but to my ears slightly awkward tune, *Because the World is Round*. I'd been trying to learn the notes for days before and could never quite get it right. On the morning I sang it five times on the walk from Holland Park tube to the rehearsal room and practically sang it back instead of saying 'hello' to the people I was introduced to. When the moment came to start the play *Because the World is Round* came out sounding distinctly unmusical. I stuck my face down into the script and quickly got on to page two.

I got through the rest of the baptism safely and we started to rehearse. Next door to the rehearsal room there was a pub where we had lunch. There was an electronic game called Pacman in the bar, which proved irresistible to Judy Holt, Jane, Alan Grint, the rest of the production team – and to me! We were soon hooked on the game of escaping the dreaded bug before it gobbled up our men. It helped us relax and get to know one another and work our way into our characters.

After two weeks' rehearsal we were scheduled to do the first filming on the serial. As it turned out, what should be my first scene on camera after ten years but the dreaded *Because the World is Round*! We did several long shots of Martin, my character, driving his car on the flyovers around Paddington. Then they constructed a camera platform on the front of the car with a light attached, stuck the sound man in beside me on the floor and told me to drive around and, on the command, start singing. It was a moment of acute embarrassment. I did it three times until everybody, including me, had had enough. The sequel to the story is that I was walking home along our street one afternoon just after the first episode had come out and my neighbour's teenage son came up.

"I enjoyed your play last night," he said.

I thanked him.

"I thought it was good the way you managed to sing out of tune on that Beatles song," he said. "It's one of my favourite records."

"But," I said, "I was trying to sing in tune."

He looked at me sympathetically. "Oh. Well, it was good anyway," he said.

Halfway through *Love Story* another call came. This time my agent was cautious.

"It's a play by Trevor Griffiths and it's not a nice character, but I think you should read it. Richard Eyre is directing."

These names meant something to me but not as much as they did to people like my brother Robert, who said they were the brilliant lights of contemporary theatre.

Richard saw me in the rehearsal rooms at Acton. He was very warm about my work and I, who had not seen any of his, felt awkward. However, I wanted to work with him on the play, which was called *Country*. He left it with me to read. It is always a great pleasure to pick up a work that speaks with authority and insight. I had to read Trevor Griffiths' play twice to fit it all together but by the second time through I was sure it was a great piece of work. The reason my agent had said that I might find my character 'not nice' was because he was homosexual.

People have asked me why I turned down *The French Lieutenant's Woman* and not *Country*. My reason was that *Country* was principally about power, wealth, background and the politics that represented them at the time of the socialist election victory in 1945. I think one reason the play was rather dismissed by some critics was that it was uncomfortably near the truth. It put the upper-middle classes under a microscope instead of on a pedestal. As an acting experince, it did worlds of good for my confidence.

Again I felt ill at ease on the first morning on location in a beautiful country house in Kent. I donned my clothes and put cream on my hair. We all had 1940s haircuts, which changed our appearances completely. Indeed when Dame Wendy Hiller saw mine, after my longish style for *Love Story*, she said, "So much better. You can see the bones."

I went outside for a Polaroid shot for continuity and inspected it to see the tell-tale grimace – a sure sign of nerves – but the double breasted suit and the setting made me feel right. Leo McKern was changing his clothes in the same room.

"It's a treat to be working with you, sir," I said.

"Oh, you say that to all the great stars," he replied.

I sauntered up into the hall where they had begun to shoot a scene between Leo McKern and Penny Wilton (my sister) into which I intruded, not having seen my sister for several years.

It went almost completely right. I stumbled over the words several times but the mood, the relationship and the character were there. It was a great feeling and the cast, director and crew were with me.

I love working with Dame Wendy, who even with her enormous wealth of experience and talent was still watching for ideas. One day she described the acting process to me perfectly – "ever a drudge and ever invigorating, ever different and ever new. That is why one is ever learning and can find it fascinating. As long as one can stand up and speak."

She said this as we were taking a stroll after we had just played a scene together.

Leo McKern showed his class so often. I remember one speech about how disappointed he was with his grandson as a possible future managing director. He was pinpoint accurate on word, meaning, intention and timing. It was like playing tennis: as has been said so often, when you are in the company of better players your own game improves unrecognisably.

One of my best experiences was playing a six-minute scene with Penny Wilton. As it happened we had spent a couple of hours together one morning in the empty make-up room just talking about the actor's life and the necessary steps towards establishing a career. It was relaxed and fun and we laughed a lot. So when it came to playing our scene we already had that communication going between us. This was important because I don't have a sister and therefore don't have that experience to draw on. It was a scene that took a lot of working through in the rehearsal period.

I was away all the week for the month of shooting and got home at weekends. I was so involved in the play that I was not much fun to live with. Mary called me Philip all the time I was making it.

When *Country* came out in October it received much acclaim and I was thrilled to collect some good reviews in work I knew I could be proud of.

Back on *The Astors* we were getting into the old age make-ups which took us four hours to put on. Lisa Harrow, who played Nancy Astor, had the greatest number of sessions but I came second with about twelve mornings' worth. The latex process involves taking an impression of your face and neck in wax, then making a mould and pouring in a rubber substance which when it is extracted forms a thin mask. This is then applied with glue right from the lower eyelids to the lower neck. After that my skilful make-up artist dabbed and painted life-like tints on to it and I came out looking like death warmed up.

So with *The Astors*, *Love Story* and *Country* the BBC

provided opportunities for my comeback to acting. In ten months I had done the equivalent of four feature films. When I had left acting I was rarely doing more than two a year. One of the greatest adjustments I had to make concerned the amount of time I was now required to be away from home and the new hours of work, often in the evenings and weekends. There was some negative reaction from Christians who felt that going back into acting involved turning my back on God, and others who knew me well found it hard to see me acting certain parts. The hardest thing for me has been to get back my confidence and relate to the world which I had been out of for so long. What else is difficult about being a Christian in the stage world? Someone said to me, "It's funny the way you're considered a bit weird for holding opinions that have been accepted in this country for fifteen hundred years."

One of my greatest thrills in the last few years has been to see Bob Dylan turn to Christ. He doesn't necessarily call himself a 'Christian' but he's a Jewish believer. The man who has had the greatest influence on the mind and the music of the pop world has now begun to teach it about its soul and its responsibility to God. I felt, listening to him, that there was every hope that one could be a good actor and a believer as well.

Meanwhile I'm still trying to make the first feature film of my comeback. It's a Russian co-production based on the life of the ballerina Anna Pavlova. I play her manager and husband Victor d'André. I'm playing a Russian because there has to be a Western actor in a major role for the film's release outside Russia. I spent four months on the film, with a week in Cuba and three weeks in Leningrad. I was very impressed by the visual splendour of Russian cinema, the crowds, the costumes, the locations all around the world. I was less impressed by their driving. In Cuba we could have been killed when our van left the road at about 60 m.p.h. at night, slid down an embankment and went for twenty-five metres along a barbed wire fence before it was finally slowed down in heavy mud near a river. The weeks away from my family, trying to act a Russian and getting used to working with Russians certainly brought back the old nervous tic again!

I suppose the big question I have tried to answer in this book is 'why did you come back to acting?' Was it, as one columnist wrote, that religion was not enough? Not in the least. My reasons are these: it's because people I meet in my world can hear the gospel, if I'm faithful; because I feel I have something to offer through my acting talent; because it's a job I enjoy.

'The same Lord is Lord of all and richly blesses all who call on him' (Romans 10:12).

Charles Colson

LIFE SENTENCE

When Charles Colson was released from prison in 1975, he simply wanted to rejoin his family and build a new life. Instead, he found himself pioneering a highly original ministry to prison inmates and campaigning for penal reform.

In 'Life Sentence' we see how Charles Colson, despite the hostility of officials and inmates alike, his faith scorned, his motives queried, has developed a Christian outreach ministry to prisons on both sides of the Atlantic.

Neil Boyd

THE HIDDEN YEARS
A novel about Jesus

Who has not wondered about Jesus' early years? His life at home, his work, his relationships with family and friends? What were his feelings about the divine mission he was to undertake?

Neil Boyd's Jesus is an arresting and vital figure. We see him at the heart of village life, watch his reactions to tragedy and suffering, learn with him and follow his steps towards the anguished struggle with the Tempter which heralds the beginning of his New Testament ministry.

NEIL BOYD is well known for the *Bless Me Father* books which have been made into a television series.

David Watson

FEAR NO EVIL

FEAR NO EVIL is a unique testimony of faith that will leave no one unmoved.

A routine visit to the doctor revealed that David Watson had cancer. Already it had spread too far to be arrested.

How he coped with such a radical turn in his life is now revealed with extraordinary courage and honesty. The stark reality of death and the question of suffering demand to be faced as never before. Faith is tested to the limit but through it all a new reliance on God emerges together with firm conviction that the best is yet to be.

David Watson is author of many best-selling titles including DISCIPLESHIP and YOU ARE MY GOD.

David Sheppard

BIAS TO THE POOR

The burden of unemployment and disadvantage falls unequally on our divided society, hitting the urban poor most sharply who are thus robbed of the freedom of choice God intends for all human beings. David Sheppard, Bishop of Liverpool, draws from thirty years' experience of urban life to issue a hard-hitting challenge: the attitudes, beliefs and priorities of the whole Church should reflect God's bias to the poor.

'The Church will not be able to ignore this book. BIAS TO THE POOR makes it clear that in David Sheppard a new William Temple has arisen.' *The Times*

Cliff Richard

WHICH ONE'S CLIFF

What is it like to be so popular that you are voted THE WORLD'S NUMBER ONE MALE SINGER? To be catapulted in a single year from teenage obscurity to top-of-the-bill celebrity?

What is it like to combine a passionate Christian faith with all the glamour and glitter of the showbiz circuit?

Once called the 'bad boy of pop' and 'too sexy for television', Cliff Richard is today acclaimed the world over as a top entertainer — yet he still finds time to visit refugee camps in Bangladesh and missionary outposts in the Sudan.

From the gossip-columns to the dirt tracks of Africa, from his public image to his private dreams, WHICH ONE'S CLIFF brings you Cliff's astonishing and engaging story in his own words.